Is GOD? Really Alive.

YES HE IS, AND HE HAS YOU
IN THE PALM OF HIS HAND

AE CHA ARROYO

ISBN 978-1-64569-069-6 (paperback)
ISBN 978-1-64569-071-9 (hardcover)
ISBN 978-1-64569-070-2 (digital)

Copyright © 2019 by Ae Cha Arroyo

All rights reserved. No part of this publication may be reproduced, distributed, or transmitted in any form or by any means, including photocopying, recording, or other electronic or mechanical methods without the prior written permission of the publisher. For permission requests, solicit the publisher via the address below.

Christian Faith Publishing, Inc.
832 Park Avenue
 Meadville, PA 16335
www.christianfaithpublishing.com

Printed in the United States of America

Contents

1	Those Ladies Said, "I Am a Sinner"	5
2	The First Miracle: Healing from Asthma	17
3	An Angel Was Standing at My Door	24
4	I Asked You to Say "Hello"	31
5	Unhappy with God: Numbers of Hair on My Head	41
6	Bug Story 1: God Saved the Drowning Bug	51
7	Bug Story 2: Bug Gives Testimony	57
8	Selling Our House: How Did I Teach You?	65
9	When Did I Say, "I Will Prosper?"	75
10	Free from Addiction: Some Interest	82
11	Pastor Black: Testing of Faith	91
12	First Job: Pray Specifically	103
13	Hepatitis C	121
14	Witness to Sunny 1: Fortune-Teller	132
15	Witness to Sunny 2: I Was Watching You	143
16	Witness to Sunny 3: God Stopped Demon's Power	153
17	Second Job: You Can Do It Again	161
18	Second Job: Don't Block Your Answers!	176
19	Are You Perfect?	188
20	Court Case: Why Did You Come to Me?	197
21	Jericho March	214
22	I No Longer Wish to Teach Her: God's Justice	221
23	"Who am I?" Jehovah Jira	239

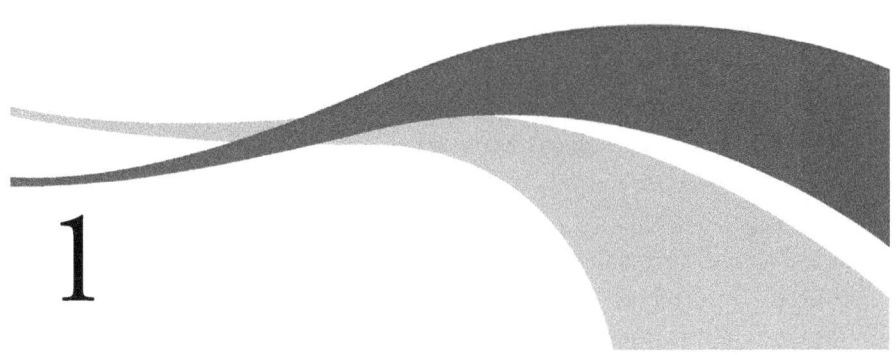

1

Those Ladies Said, "I Am a Sinner"

After my husband finished his tour of duty in South Korea, he received a new assignment to the State of Missouri. We moved into military housing at 16 Totten Street on the military base. It was there that I was invited by, not from one church, but from four different Korean churches. These sisters kept coming back to my house to invite me to their church. They took turns stopping by nearly every day for about two months.

Sometimes, when I was out shopping, someone would have stopped by and dropped off different kinds of food on my front door step. Oftentimes, I didn't know which sister dropped this off for us. Everything began to annoy me. Many times, I told them not come to our house, but they kept on coming!

I got so annoyed by the entire situation, I decided, once for all, I wanted to end the whole thing forever! I thought about it for a while to decide what I need to do and how I must do it to bring this to an end. Then, I had a few strategies to end the entire situation.

One of my strategies was to tell three different church sisters that I've made a choice as to which church I would go to, and it would be the Presbyterian church. Just as I thought, that strategy did work! Minutes after I told them what I had decided to do, all of them stopped coming to my house except the Presbyterians sisters! But what these sisters didn't know was I had a plan for them also. My plan was, after two Sunday visits to church, I was not going to go back to the church.

Now, I had couple of reasons why I chose the Presbyterian church. One reason was the sisters from that church were quite young as I was, and I thought they would handle disappointment far better than the sisters from other churches. If I attended church for only two Sundays and stopped afterwards, the sisters from other churches, who were much older, might feel hurt and disappointed.

Another reason I chose Presbyterian church was a sister from that church said a couple of things that touched my heart. One particular sister consistently told me, "You are a sinner. God is remembering all your sins, and you need His forgiveness."

This same sister also told me, after she received Jesus as her "Savior", her marriage changed and she's far happier with her husband than ever before!

This testimony really touched my heart! At that time, I felt like I was in a miserable marriage. I was only thirty-two, but I was extremely unhappy with my marriage. Therefore, her testimony was another reason why I chose to go to the Presbyterian church. But remember, I still planned to go to the church for only two Sundays.

On Sunday morning, a sister came to pick me up for church. When I arrived at the church, they gave me a bible and a hymnal book as a gift. As the service started, The Pastor asked the congregation to pray. I bowed my head to pray, but I didn't know what to pray. Then I remembered what a sister told me, "You are a sinner, and God remembers all your sins." So, I decided to pray to find out whether God remembered all my sins or not.

I thought if He is real, then He should remember all my sins, as she had said. So, I prayed. "God, those ladies, who are sitting over there, told me I am a sinner and you remember all my sins. If you are real and remember all my sins, reveal it to me." Then I lifted my head and saw that everyone was still praying, so I bowed my head again and repeated the same prayer. I repeated it many times as the pastor ended the prayers. (He prayed through a microphone).

I made this prayer because if God is real and remembered all my sins, He certainly shouldn't have any difficulty to reveal it to me. If He can do that, then I know He is real. And if God is real, I will serve Him, but if He is not real, I was not going to allow anyone to talk to me about God at all. That was the reason why I prayed that prayer. After I came home, I said to myself, "Well, only next Sunday. After that, I am done with church for a long time. If He is real, I will serve God when I am old."

The following Sunday, I rode with a sister who came to pick me up. As the church service started, the same things happened as the previous Sunday. The pastor asked the congregation to bow their heads and pray. I prayed the same thing. "God, those ladies, who sit over there, told me I am a sinner and you remember all my sins. If you are real and remember all my sins, reveal it to me."

Then I lifted my head to look around, and the people were still praying. I felt awkward because I didn't know where to put my eyes on, so I bowed my head again and repeated the same prayer many times until the pastor ended his prayer.

After the service, I came home and said to myself, "I am done with the church. This is it. If I do serve God, I will serve Him when I am old but not now."

I thought that everything worked perfectly for me. I got rid of all the other church sisters and the only sisters left for me to get rid of were the Presbyterians. I thought about what I was going to say to the sister who would call to pick me up for next Sunday service. I said to myself, "When she calls, I will let her know that I am done with the church. I will tell her, I will serve God later but not now." That was my plan.

That Sunday evening, I went to my bedroom to sleep. As I laid down, I noticed a tiny shape of a maple leaf on the ceiling. It looked like a tiny infant's hand with five fingers. Its print was very vivid, but it looked so odd to me because I never saw anything like that before. So, I closed my eyes for a moment and opened them to look at the ceiling.

I expected to see nothing, but it got a little bigger! I felt very strange and quickly thought, *Maybe, my eyes must be very tired.* The second time, I closed my eyes a little longer and opened them to look at the ceiling. To my big surprise, it grew bigger than the last time! It got bigger as a big man's hand, and its print was very clear.

I got a little frightened and I sat in an upright position and closed my eyes even longer than the last time and opened them again. Instead of looking at the ceiling, this time, I decided to look at the floor. I was a little frightened to look at the celling. I expected to see nothing because, I thought, maybe, something was on the ceiling. Then, when I looked at the floor, it appeared there too! I got terrified even more.

I was hoping to see nothing, but what I hoped was wrong. It was as big as one foot wide, and its print was very strong. I looked at the ceiling, but it wasn't there but on the floor. Now my husband even noticed something was wrong! He asked, "What's wrong?" I didn't give him an answer. I just told him to be quiet.

Then I closed my eyes again. This time, I made sure I closed my eyes longer than any other time. I opened my eyes and looked on the floor. Again, it grew to double in size, as almost two feet in diameter.

I got very terrified but didn't know what to do. My husband kept asking me what was wrong. As I got up from bed, I told him what I was seeing and asked him to look at the floor. Of course, he couldn't see anything, but from my reaction, he also got frightened. Then he grabbed the phone and dialed to call his mother—she was a devout Christian.

At the same time, I grabbed my Bible. I didn't even know why I put a Bible on my nightstand, but it was there. I began to flip its pages as fast as I could, but I didn't know what I was looking for. I just flipped it as fast as I could to find some scriptures. Then I realized it was useless. I have never read a Bible and didn't even know what scriptures I was supposed to look for or find.

I gave up flipping pages and put my whole face into the Bible and made this confession repeatedly: "I will serve you, I will serve you. God, please help me. I will serve you, I will serve you. God, please help me." I didn't know how many times I repeated this to God.

I said this to God because somehow, I suspected, God was doing this to me. Somehow, I felt, He didn't like the decision I made about church and Him. Therefore, God wanted to frighten me for making a wrong choice about serving Him. I made that confession based upon what I felt.

Then all of a sudden, my husband handed me the phone to talk to his mom. I didn't know what conversation they had. I said, "Hello." She asked, "Did you get invited to church?" "Yes," I told her how I was invited to church and how many times I went to church. Then she told me, "God is calling you. You shouldn't reject Him. You must serve Him. You need to go the church." I told her I will, then I hung up the phone and looked at the floor and at the ceiling. Magically, there was no imprint at both places! It was gone!

Well, this was how God had taken the Christian journey for me. I went to church the following Sunday with the sister from the church. This was my third Sunday service onto the Lord. I repeated the same prayer. "God, those ladies who sit over there told me I am a sinner and you remember all my sins. If you are real and remember all my sins, reveal it to me." I prayed like this every time I went to church service.

Prayers were not the only thing I did. I also read the Bible as much as I could to find out whether He is real or not. If He is real, I wanted to find out for myself. I didn't want to base my faith according to what someone had said. Therefore, every opportunity I got, I read, read, and read. Oftentimes, I read until 3:00 or 4:00 a.m. and still got up at the same time as usual to take care of my children, and whenever I found any time to read, I read, read, and read.

About three months of going to church, God began to answer my prayers. I started to get convictions of my sins. He started to remind me of my sins—sins that I completely forgot about for a long time. As a matter of fact, not only did I forget, if I did remember, I was not feeling guilty of my sins because I had good excuses for my sins. So, whenever I did remember the sins, I justified all my sins.

But, oh yes, He remembered all my sins just as that lady had said! One by one, God brought sins to my attention. As He reminded me of my sins, one by one, I had to ask God for forgiveness.

I will share with you one example. One day, I was cleaning the dishes in the kitchen, and all of a sudden, God reminded me about the sweet rice donut I stole when I was nine years old. At that time in Korea, school supplies stores were located right in front of the school entrance.

These stores also sold many snacks, toys, and all kinds of popular things children might be interested to buy. If children needed to buy school supplies and other things, parents gave them money to buy from these stores. Of course, rich children came to school with more money to spend than poorer children.

One recess time, I went to the store with a bunch of other kids. We ran to the store with excitement. Everyone was shouting, talking, kidding, and making all kinds of noises. This store displayed a few different types of snacks outside of the store, including the donuts.

With a bunch kids yelling, talking, and asking the store owner how much certain things cost, I saw a donut hole size of sweet rice donut. I asked her how much it cost, but I didn't have any money. I was very hungry, and when I looked at the store owner, she was very busy with the other children. At that moment, I took the donut and put it to my mouth and ate it.

Then moments later, she asked, "Hey, didn't you eat a donut?" With that question, everyone looked at me. I was very scared. I told her no. Then she had a puzzled look on her face, moved her head side to side for she wasn't sure whether I ate it or not, and then she moved on to another kid. I thought, *Phew, what a relief.*

At that very moment, I had a great relief and had this very thought, *Wow, what if I was caught? It would had been big disaster. I will never do this again. I will never steal again.* But instead of feeling guilty, I was very happy that I didn't get caught. If I would have been caught, I would possibly have been tagged as a "thief girl" for rest of my school life.

Anyway, because I was so glad that I didn't get caught, I quickly forget about it for years! But He remembered all my sins. If God didn't bring it to my attention, I probably would have never remembered it at all, but God remembered everything. God is faithful. He answered me as I prayed.

Additionally, not only did He remind me of all the sins I committed, God also helped me to look at my emotional sins through the Bible. Sins of pride, arrogance, hatred, bitterness, resentment, anger, unforgiveness, and many more. These kinds of sins, I couldn't notice easily because it was hidden deep inside my heart. I was like a whitewashed tomb full of dead men's bones and all uncleanliness (Matthew 23:27).

As He revealed my inner sins to me, I began to confess and ask for cleanliness. Do you know what? I always believed, I was a pretty good person until God revealed all my sins to me. Wow, what a great sinner I was. I didn't know, I needed that much forgiveness!

This incident helped me to realize God is truly alive and remembers all sins until one asks for forgiveness. It also helped me to understand how much I had been forgiven, what has been forgiven, and why Jesus had to die for me. What Jesus had to suffer for my sins and how he suffered for a great sinner like me, so that I could be forgiven and reconciled with God the Father.

This instance helped me to deeply appreciate Him for His love, suffering on the cross, and the resurrection of Jesus. Since that time, I never walked away from God. Now I am a minister of Jesus Christ who teaches people about our "Savior of the World".

Now, I want to share with you what I have learned. Over time, I have met many people who confessed Jesus Christ as their Lord and Savior and go to church regularly, but I have realized one thing about some of them. They didn't really understand who Jesus is to them and what's been forgiven.

They say, they are thankful for what Jesus has done for them, but their testimony of life is very ungrateful. They are very judgmental, critical, not quick to forgive, and have a weak faith in Jesus. If they really understood their sins had been forgiven by the suffering of Jesus, they would have a very hard time to demand their debts to be paid for them.

Oh, but how many people I met who are so judgmental, so critical, so unforgiving, so ungrateful, and so unfaithful to Jesus. Almost certainly, they act this way because they never truly recognized themselves as a sinner who was forgiven by Jesus.

> Jesus answered him, "Simon, I have something to tell you." "Tell me, teacher," he said. "Two people owed money to a certain moneylender. One owed him five hundred denarii, and the other fifty. Neither of them had the money to pay him back, so he forgave the debts of both. Now which of them will love him more?" Simon replied, "I suppose the one who had the bigger debt forgiven." "You have judged correctly," Jesus said… Therefore, I tell you, her many sins have been forgiven—as her great love has shown. But whoever has been forgiven little loves little.
>
> (Luke 7:40–43, 47; NIV)

This parable has nothing do with the quantity of sins. If it were so, we all must commit more sins and greater sins to obtain more forgiveness. Jesus is talking about the deep honest realization of sins and confession of these sins.

> "But I tell you that anyone who looks at a woman lustfully has already committed adultery with her in his heart."
>
> (Matthew 5:28, NIV)

Let's say two men looked at the woman lustfully and committed adultery in their heart. One realized he committed adultery by looking at the woman lustfully and confessed it to Jesus to receive forgiveness, but the other thinks, as long as he didn't physically lay with the woman, it is not a sin. Therefore, he feels he doesn't need to confess to receive forgiveness.

But just as the first man, the more you realize your sins, the more you will confess to Jesus, and the more you confess, the more you will receive forgiveness. Then the more you realize how many debts have been forgiven, the more you realize how precious Jesus is to you, and the more you love Jesus, and people. But if you acknowledge only a few sins, confess only a few, and receive forgiveness for a few, then your love and gratitude remains small toward Jesus and people. This is what Jesus meant in: "But whoever has been forgiven little loves little."

> "The Law came in so that the transgression would increase; but where sin increased, grace abounded all the more."
>
> (Romans 5:20, NASB)

"But where sin increased, grace abounded all the more" again, it doesn't mean we should go around committing more transgressions to increase our sins so grace is to be abound. This scripture is simply talking about more laws were added to define more transgressions to one to realize what sin is.

The more one realizes what sin is, the more one confesses to Jesus, and then the grace of Jesus will abound all the more to this individual who realizes more sins and confesses more. Therefore, grace abounded all the more to a sin conscience's heart.

My sins were not heavier, nor bigger, nor many more than everyone's sins. I didn't murder anyone, which is consider the biggest sins, in human terms. I committed sins just as anyone would have committed. If I may say, "very ordinary sins," which everyone in the world commits. Lying, cheating, fighting, cursing, etc.

But I am not more righteous than a murderer. I give all the praise to God that I had a great opportunity to ask Him to reveal all my sins to me, which were many, and His answer to help me deeply realize how much Jesus had to suffer for my sins, and His grace *abounded all the more* for my sins. "Praise the Lord."

You see, some pastors say it is not good to remember your sins. They teach that Jesus forgave all our sins; therefore, we don't need to remember our sins and just move on with life. Yes, indeed, Jesus forgave us of all our sins. That's true, but I beg to differ. If you just accepts forgiveness, this will not help you to understand what has been forgiven, how much has been forgiven for you, why Jesus had to suffer for your sins, how much He suffered for your sins, and how much of your debts has been paid by Jesus.

> Surely, He has borne our griefs And carried our sorrows; Yet we esteemed Him stricken, Smitten by God, and afflicted. But He was wounded for our transgressions, He was bruised for our iniquities; The chastisement for our peace was upon Him, And by His stripes we are healed… He poured out His soul unto death, And He was numbered with the transgressors, And He bore the sin of many And made intercession for the transgressors.
>
> (Isaiah 53:4–5, 12b; NKJV)

You may say you understand these scriptures, but if you didn't see His crucifixion through the forgiveness of your sins, you may not really understand. It is very different for one to acknowledge the scripture than experiencing the scriptures. And anyone who experience His suffering, His wounds, His bruises, His chastisement, His stripes through experience of forgiveness of sins, above scriptures, Isaiah 53:4–5 and 12 will become a reality.

His crucifixion is absolutely real, but if you never saw your sins, you can't understand. You can't have any real idea what has been forgiven and how much has been forgiven. Jesus's crucifixion is not easy to understand if you never saw your physical and emotional sins. If you didn't see your sins and acknowledge what has been forgiven, His death cannot be a reality to you. Only through acknowledgment of sins, confession of the sins, and forgiveness of sins, His crucifixion truly can be understood.

Without seeing my sins, I would not have understood Isaiah 53—His death, His suffering, His wounds, His bruises, His chastisement, His stripes, and His love. Seeing my sins helped me to understand why Jesus had to die for me, why he had to suffer for me, and how much He loved me to die for me. It is okay to believe and accept you are forgiven, but this in itself will not help you to understand who Jesus Christ is to you.

The more you realize what Jesus had suffered to forgive you, the more you will understand Jesus. The more you'll be thankful to Jesus, the more you'll be humble to Jesus, and you'll become less judgmental, critical, and quick to forgive. Therefore, acknowledgment of your sins and confession of your sins is not condemning; it is about acknowledging the need of His forgiveness, His mercies, and His love.

Furthermore, just accepting forgiveness will not help to improve your relationship with Jesus. You cannot develop any relationship with someone whom you don't know. Can you trust anyone that you don't know? How can you trust someone you don't know? Can you? How can anyone have confidence about someone they don't know? Can you have confidence in someone you don't know? Can you?

If you don't know who Jesus is to you, you can't trust Jesus. This is the reason why many suffer for lack of faith. If you don't know how Jesus has loved you, what he had to suffer to love you, you can't have confidence about Jesus. You can't have faith in Jesus. But if you realize how He has loved you, what He had to suffered to love you, you will have all the confidence about Jesus. You will really, truly have all the confidence in this very scripture.

> "He who did not spare his own Son, but gave him up for us all—how will he not also, along with him, graciously give us all things?"
> (Romans 8:32, NIV)

Do you want to experience Jesus's love? Do you want to develop a deep relationship with Jesus? I strongly recommend you ask God to reveal your sins to you, just as I did. Don't be afraid to ask God. You will be very surprised to find out what has been forgiven and how much has been forgiven. As a matter of fact, don't you want to know why Jesus had to suffer for you? Take an opportunity to truly understand how Jesus has loved you. You won't know until you ask what has been forgiven and how much has been forgiven.

The more you realize your sins, the more you'll understand His love for you, and you'll love Jesus all the more. I am not saying you don't love Jesus, but if you truly and deeply understand how Jesus has loved you, it will help to deepen your relationship with Jesus.

Through this experience, you'll find out how Jesus draws very close to you and you to Jesus. The depth of your relationship with Jesus Christ will be very different than ever before! Your faith will grow stronger, you'll have no doubt about Jesus. You will know for sure—absolutely know for sure—Jesus is alive and how He cares for you.

> Two people owed money to a certain moneylender. One owed him five hundred denarii, and the other fifty. Neither of them had the money to pay him back, so he forgave the debts of both. Now which of them will love him more? Simon replied, "I suppose the one who had the bigger debt forgiven." You have judged correctly," Jesus said… Therefore, I tell you, her many sins have been forgiven—as her great love has shown. But whoever has been forgiven little loves little.
> (Luke 7:41–43, 47 NIV)

Please learn to realize how much has been forgiven.

As God is alive, His word is alive. And His "Word" will prove to you, He is alive.

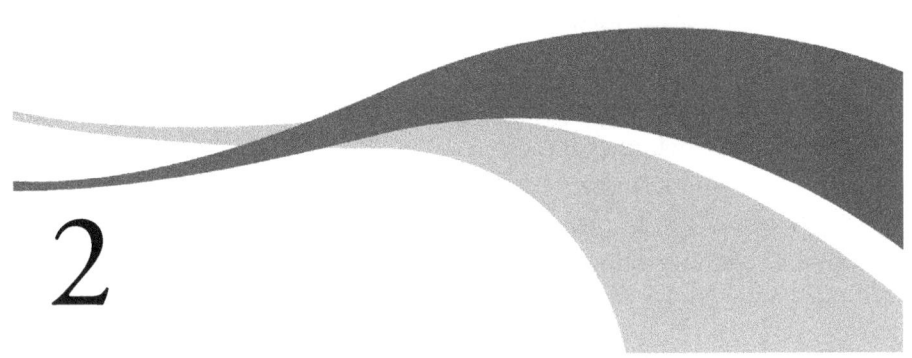

2

The First Miracle: Healing from Asthma

At this time, I had been attending church for about six months and was hooked on reading the Bible. I read it all the time. I read it anywhere and at any time. I read it when I was in the bathroom, in the kitchen while I was cooking, in the living room. I even stayed up all night until the next morning, 3:00 or 4:00 a.m., to read.

At this time, I read the entire Bible three times, from Genesis to Revelation, in a relatively short amount of time. While I was reading the Bible entirely for the fourth time, I opened it to the book of John and came across this verse.

> "Whatever you ask in My name, that will I do,
> so that the Father may be glorified in the Son. If
> you ask Me anything in My name, I will do it."
> (John 14:13–14, NASB)

It shocked me because I read this scripture before, and it didn't mean anything to me back then. It was just a word. It didn't have any impact on me whatsoever, but this time, it said something very different to me. The word popped out at me like a bullet shot from a gun, and it penetrated my heart. For some reason, this time was very different than before.

I was wondering about this particular scripture: *"Ask anything in His name?"* and *"then He will do it?"* With this thought in my mind, I kept on reading to the next chapter—15 and on to 16—until I ran into a similar scripture again!

> In that day you will not question Me about anything. Truly, truly, I say to you, if you ask the Father for anything in My name, He will give it to you. Until now you have asked for nothing in My name; ask and you will receive, so that your joy may be made full.
>
> (John 16:23–24, NASB)

When I ran into these scriptures, I stopped reading and asked myself a question. "Wow, if I ask anything in His name He will give to me? Whatever I ask? What should I ask from God then? Should I ask God for money?" My answer was no, because God will not rain down money on me. God will provide more money through the natural process. Either I need to ask God to provide a job for me, or ask God to promote my husband to earn more money.

But at this point in our lives, either way was not the way to receive more money from God. Since money was not the one thing I would ask from God, I sat on the bed to ponder what I should ask God.

After I ran into those scriptures, I had no doubt in my mind that God would give me whatever I asked in His Name. *But what? What should I ask from God?*

Then all of sudden, I heard this voice from within me. "Why don't you ask for your husband's healing?" I said, "Huh, ask for my husband's healing?" I didn't know it was the voice of the Lord. I never heard His voice before. This was the first time I ever heard the voice of God. Therefore, I didn't know how to recognize His voice. Just like the prophet Samuel (1 Samuel 3).

When Samuel was living with the prophet Eli, the boy Samuel heard God calling him three times, but Samuel didn't know it was the voice of God until Eli told him what to say to God. I was in the same spiritual position. This was the first time I heard the voice of God but had no way of recognizing it. Therefore, I did not pay too much attention to it. I thought, I was hearing my own conscience.

However, I immediately thought this was very good idea to ask God for my husband's healing. At that time, my husband was dealing with chronic asthma. So, I began to pray exactly like this: "Father, I thank you for protecting my family today. God, your word says that if I ask anything in the name of Jesus, you will give it to me. So I am asking you to heal my husband's asthma. In the name of Jesus, amen." That was all I said to God.

The next day, during the evening, before I read my Bible, I prayed the same way as I did the night before. "Father, I thank you for protecting my family today," and said, "God, your word says if I ask anything in the name of Jesus, you will give it to me. So I pray to you to heal my husband's asthma. In the name of Jesus, amen." That was all I said to God for three nights. I did not say anything else but that simple prayer.

On the fourth night, when I was praying for my husband's healing, I heard this voice within me, "Child, your husband is healed." Well, I didn't even know that this was the answer from the Lord. The next night, I repeated the same prayer to God and the Lord told me, "Child, you don't need to pray for that anymore. He is healed." Again, I didn't understand this was an answer from God.

On the next night, I just forget to pray for my husband's healing. I didn't really know why I did not pray, but I just didn't pray for his healing anymore. Perhaps, because I heard what God had said about his healing.

Anyway, I didn't know it was God's voice until a few days later. One early evening, one of the sisters from the church stopped by to visit me. We were enjoying each other's personal testimonies—mostly, I enjoyed her testimonies. I began to share with her my testimony about how I got blessed by reading John 14:13 and 16:23, and how I prayed to God each night according to these scriptures.

Then suddenly, a thought jumped from within me and I said to her, "Wait a minute! Wait a minute! I think I got an answer from

God!" I shouted, "When I was praying on the fourth and fifth night, I heard this voice saying that God healed my husband."

At that very moment, I knew in my heart I had received an answer from the Lord! At that very moment, I knew for sure that my husband was healed. I knew for sure I heard the voice of God for the first time! I was so excited, so happy, that I started jumping up and down for a little while because of the joy in my heart.

From that moment, I couldn't wait until my husband got home from work in order to confirm it. I just could not wait until my husband came home because I wanted to find out for sure. Well, about thirty minutes later, my husband walked in the house.

Without saying "hello" or "how was your day", I just asked him a point-blank question. No! perhaps, more like I was shouting at him. My question to him was more like I was attacking him, "Have you been taking your asthma medicine?" He hesitated to answer for a moment like he didn't know how to answer. Then he asked, "Why do you want to know?"

He had a perplexed look on his face. He looked as though he was trying to figure out in his mind why I asked such a question. Again, I asked him, "Have you been taking your asthma medicine lately?" With a puzzled look on his face, he said no. Then I asked, "Why not?"

"Well? Because I did not feel any pain in breathing. I was able to breath without any medication!"

"How long ago did you stop taking your medication?"

"Well, I stopped taking it a few days ago?!"

"When was that?"

"Well, about three or four days ago?"

Even though he was answering all my questions, he didn't have any idea why I was asking him all of these questions and had puzzled look on his face. Then he asked, "Why are you asking me all these questions?" Then I told him, "You are healed from asthma!" Then he said, "What? How do you know that?"

Then I sat down with him and explained what had happened. I told him he was healed. And the reason why he didn't have any difficulty in breathing because he received his healing from God.

He was shocked, but at the same time, he thanked God for what God did for him. Ever since that time, my husband never has taken any medication for his breathing.

Well, let's think about it for a moment and realize just how good God is. I did not do anything to receive this healing from God. I just believed what the scripture says and prayed in the name of Jesus to receive this wonderful gift from God. God honored my faith, and He honored His words. I didn't pray long for hours or with lengthy prayers, and I didn't fast for days; I just prayed for a few seconds. Perhaps, only one minute? That's all.

Some people think that they need to pray for an hour or longer to receive an answer from God, but the only thing you need to do is to believe in His Word. You may pray for many hours and many days, but it will not work until you believe what He promised in His Word.

> "If you abide in Me, and My words abide in you, you will ask what you desire, and it shall be done for you."
>
> (John 15:7, NKJV)

The scripture says if you belong to Jesus and if God's promise is in you, you should ask whatever you desire. How wonderful a promise this is. As long as you belong to Him and as long as you believe in His promises, you can ask whatever you desire. That's exactly what I did. I knew for sure that I belonged to Him, and then all of a sudden, when reading His Word, the word got in me. His Word was abiding in me (John 14:13 and 16:23).

The Bible says, "Faith come from hearing of His word!" (Romans 10:17). I heard the word while I was reading His Word—the Bible. I heard His Word through my eyes. I didn't do anything special. I just read my Bible quietly, then my spirit heard it, and my faith came from hearing of the word. When my spirit heard the word of God, my spirit was in agreement with the word. That was all. I just read and asked according to what I heard in my spirit, asked according to His word that abide in me.

Without His Word, you don't have anything to base your faith on. You must have His Word in you in order to ask God according to His promises. Without knowing the word and believing His Word, you don't know what to ask from God. I want to encourage you to spend time with His Word. Either through reading your Bible or listening to an audio Bible or reading on your smart phone or tablet. If you can believe His Word, you are guaranteed to receive an answer from God.

> "My covenant I will not break, Nor alter the word that has gone out of My lips. Once I have sworn by My holiness; I will not lie to David: [insert your name in here]."
> (Psalm 89:34–35, NKJV)

Whatever promises you can believe, He will not break it. Whatever promises you can believe, He will not alter it. He will answer your faith because His promises are sworn by His holiness.

What are you going through right now? Or what do you need from God right now? Ask anything in Jesus's name. This is a promise from the Lord. If you can believe these scriptures as I did, and if you ask God like I did, you will receive answers from God, like I did.

> Whatever you ask in My name, that will I do, so that the Father may be glorified in the Son. If you ask Me anything in My name, I will do it.
> (John 14:13–14, NASB)

> In that day you will not question Me about anything. Truly, truly, I say to you, if you ask the Father for anything in My name, He will give it to you. Until now you have asked for nothing in My name; ask and you will receive, so that your joy may be made full.
> (John 16:23–24, NASB)

Can you believe these scriptures Like I believed? If you do believe, ask God for whatever you need from Him. If these words abide in you, ask. It will be done for you.

You will experience Jesus's name is the most powerful name. You will experience Jesus is truly alive.

As God is alive, His word is alive. And His "Word" will prove to you, He is alive.

3

An Angel Was Standing at My Door

As I sat down to pray, I closed my eyes and I saw an angel standing at the room door! I heard about angels, but I never saw one in my life. This was the very first time I saw an angel. The angel was about seven feet tall and had on a very long and comfortable size bright white linen robe.

As I began to pray, the angel dropped his hands and lifted each side of his robe to make a huge pouch, like a kangaroo pouch. That pouch was to collect my prayers and take it to God. When I noticed this, I was very happy and excited. "Wow, an angel is taking my prayers to God. Wow."

So, I prayed louder and faster as I could. Since that moment, every time I sat down to pray, I saw an angel standing at the door and did the same thing—gathering my prayers into the pouch to take it to God. This went on for a while.

One day, as usual, I sat down to pray, but I couldn't see the angel. I thought, *Maybe just this time.* At first, I didn't even notice it. Just one day, I happened to notice I couldn't see the angel.

It began to bother me. Some thoughts were bubbling up within me. *Did I do something wrong? What is going on? What happened to the angel?* I was wondering, *If the angel is not taking my prayers to God, then who is taking my prayers to God? Who? And where are my prayers going? To no one? To nowhere?*

Though I had all these thoughts, I still prayed every day. But I felt like I didn't pray because I had all these questions. I couldn't concentrate on prayer because I was looking for an angel. I did not remember what I prayed because I placed all my attention looking for an angel rather than focusing on praying. It bothered me so deeply that I completely lost the joy of prayer. Prayer didn't make me happy anymore. I struggled with praying every day, and this went on for about three months.

As usual, I sat down to pray, and all of a sudden, God asked me, "When are you going to start believing my Word?" I thought, *What does this mean,* Again God asked, "When are you going to start to believe my Word?" I paused and didn't say anything because I didn't understand what God was asking.

God continued, "Even though you cannot see the angel, don't you know that I am still hearing your prayers?" God repeated, "Don't you know I am still hearing your prayers?" At that very moment, I realized what a huge mistake I had made. Realizing my mistake, I said, "Oh my god!"

I lost the joy of praying because I expected to see the angel rather than believe God's Word! Before I saw the angel, I just believed His Word and prayed. I prayed without any doubt. I had much joy in praying because I had faith in God's Word. I just simply believed His Word when praying, but after I saw the angel, I got completely distracted. I expected to see an angel every time I prayed.

When I realized I couldn't see the angel anymore, I began to doubt. I doubted that God was not hearing my prayers. Because I can't see an angel anymore, I thought and believed my prayers were not reaching the Father. I completely forgot what God said. He said if we call upon Him, He hears us but I got distracted by what I saw. I lost focus to believe His Word. I lost all joy of praying because I was expecting to see an angel rather than believe His words.

> "Therefore, angels are only servants—spirits sent to care for people who will inherit salvation."
> (Hebrews 1:14, NLT)

God's Word says that angels are sent to the saints to serve as ministering spirits. Whether I see an angel or not, the angel is always with me to serve me. Whether I could see angel or not, the angel is always taking my prayers to the Father. I forgot about this very important fact because of what I saw.

Vision of God Is for Specific Purpose

In the Bible, God showed spiritual visions to His people through an angel. God shows spiritual realms of things to His people according to His will and for specific purposes, but once His will and purpose has been fulfilled or satisfied, the vision stopped.

For example, in Acts 10, an angel of God appeared to Cornelius and gave specific instructions to invite Peter to his house. The next day, when Peter went on the rooftop to pray, the vision of God appeared to Peter. This vision appeared to Peter three times, and Peter didn't have any understanding about the vision.

When people from Cornelius came looking for Peter, the Spirit of the Lord told Peter to go with them without any doubts or hesitation. Peter went with them without understanding the vision, but when Peter entered Cornelius's house, he understood the vision.

> "Then Peter opened his mouth and said: "In truth I perceive that God shows no partiality. But in every nation whoever fears Him and works righteousness is accepted by Him."
> (Acts. 10:34–35, NKJV)

Peter preached to them about Jesus and the salvation of the Lord. All the people with Cornelius that day got saved, filled with the Holy Spirit, and spoke in heavenly tongues. The vison of God was fulfilled and satisfied. Once that vision was done, it never reappeared to Peter nor an angel of God to Cornelius.

In Acts 9, Paul, his name previously was Saul before he got converted, was traveling to Damascus to capture Christians. While he was on the road, he saw a vision and lost his eyesight. He was led by his companions to Damascus. For three days and three nights, he couldn't drink nor eat.

Then the Lord appeared to Ananias in a vision to show what was needed to be done to help Paul. Paul also saw in a vision Ananias placing his hands on him to restore Paul's sight.

Ananias went to Paul and placed his hand on him to recover Paul's sight as they saw in a vision. Through this event, Paul realized Jesus is the Lord and savior of the world and his calling on his life. This vison was fulfilled and never again appeared to both Paul and Ananias.

As we just saw in the Bible, many visions had been revealed to God's people—the spiritual realm of things and its purpose—but all these visions were different from one another. Once the vision was understood by his people and after the vision had been fulfilled, the vision was not shown to the people anymore. If there is any other purpose for His will, God will reveal His vision to his people to carry out His purpose.

The Occult

There is one thing, we must make sure absolutely right about regarding visions. Man does not control the "vision", but God does. He is the one who controls all heavenly visions. He determines how, when, what, and to whom the vision is revealed. There are groups of people who gather together to pray just to see a vision. They all fall on the floor, screaming, shouting, shaking, and twitching their bodies just to see a vision. They talk as though they are the ones who control the vision, like turning a light switch on and off.

They claimed every time they pray that their spirit enters a spiritual realm to receive the vision. The vision they saw didn't have any purpose, nor the will of the Father, but just using this to brag how spiritual they are to the immature Christians.

People who are involved in this type of group don't even know this is false. They are deceived. Without any questions or objections, they follow false leaders blindly because of their ignorance of scripture. Some baby Christian becomes envious and want to do the same thing.

You need to be very careful about the occult. In this kind of cult, if you say, you can't see the vision, then they say it is because you are not that spiritual. Don't let them disqualify your spirituality.

> "Let no one disqualify you, insisting on ascetic practices and the worship of angels, claiming access to a visionary realm and inflated without cause by his unspiritual mind."
> (Colossians 2:18, HCSB)

They teach people to pray like they pray, scream like they scream, shake their body like they shake, twitch like they twitch, then they should be able to enter the spiritual realm as they please and see the vision. This is not from God! This is demonic! These are demons just mimicking God to show the vision. Satan mimics God to entice people in order to keep them away from the truth and God.

> "No wonder, for even Satan disguises himself as an angel of light. And no wonder! For Satan himself transforms himself into an angel of light."
> (2 Corinthians 11:14, NASB)

Just remember, you can't control the vision; only God can do this! You can't control the spiritual realm like turning a light switch on and off. It is not for you to decide to see the vision. God is the one decides who sees the vision. Read and study the entire Bible. You will find out God is the one who has all authority and ultimate power to decide how, when, what, and to whom He reveals the vision. If any of you are involved in this kind of group, please you need to get out of there as quickly as possible.

The vision I saw about an angel, God had a purpose. His purpose was, He didn't want me to "think" there might be an angel, but He wanted me to know for sure there are angels. He wanted me to know for sure; He sent an angel to minister to His people. God showed me my angel so I would understand why my angel was sent to me and how my angel ministers to me. That was the purpose why He allowed me to see an angel.

With this understanding, I totally got set free! I no longer struggled to pray. Though I no longer see an angel, I recovered all the joy of my prayers. From that moment, I learned to trust God's Word even more. I've learned it didn't matter what I could see or hear, I have the everlasting and unchanging promises—Words from God. His Words are more than enough for all believers.

God simply asks us to believe His Word and add faith into His Word. His Word is God Himself. God and His Word are one. If you believe His Word, then you are believing Him. God's promised to us—if we pray in Jesus's name, He will hear us and answer us. That promise I have believed.

> "And whatever you ask in My name, that I will do, that the Father may be glorified in the Son."
> (John 14:13, NKJV)

> "Ask, and it will be given to you."
> (Matthew 7:7, NKJV)

I pray that you don't make the same mistake as I did. Don't depend on your faith by what you see or hear, or what you saw, or heard. Just believe His Word. This is called faith.

> "For we walk by faith, not by sight."
> (2 Corinthians 5:7, NKJV)

> "Therefore know that only those who are of faith are sons of Abraham."
>
> (Galatians 3:7, NKJV)

Walking by faith is far more trustworthy than walking by sight. What you see or hear can be of the devil. The devil can mimic God to show you things to deceive you. Therefore, there is no guarantee of what you see or hear is of God. But the Word of God is written in the Bible, and He spoke it, and settled it in heaven forever.

> "Your word, Lord, is eternal; it stands firm in the heavens."
>
> (Psalm 119:89, NIV)

Everything will perish but not the Word of God. Don't try to see or hear something to believe God. Just trust the Word of God. His Word lasts forever! His Word is forever settled in heaven.

If you are the person who always want to see or hear things to believe, God is now asking you, "When are you going to start to believe my Word?"

As God is alive, His word is alive. And His "Word" will prove to you, He is alive.

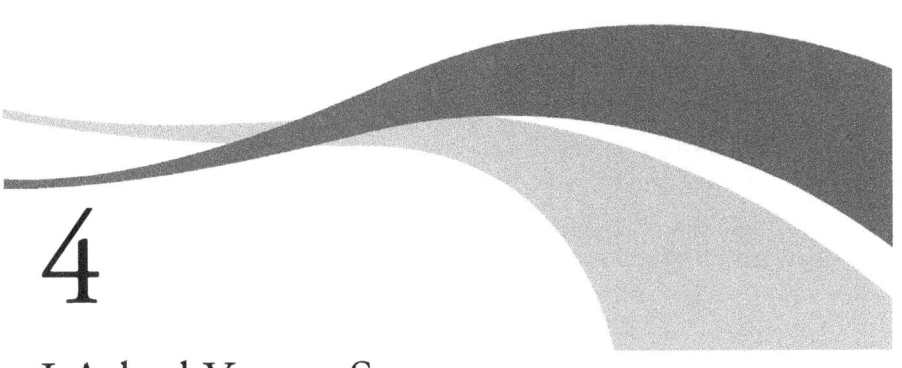

4

I Asked You to Say "Hello"

While we were living in Missouri, my husband and I decided to change our home church to better fit our growing family. We decided to attend one of the local churches that was well known to many people in the area we lived. One Sunday, we visited this well-known church, and we ran into a couple we knew as acquaintance.

They recognized us just as we recognized them. We were happy to run into them because we didn't know anyone else in that church. We said "hello" to each other and exchanged small talk. We enjoyed the service, and we decided to attend that church as our home church.

After attending this church for a few Sundays, I happened to notice something very strange about this lady whom I knew. Every Sunday when I saw her, I wanted to acknowledge her by greeting her, but she acted as though she didn't want me to notice her at all.

After service, I told my husband how she acted toward me, then my husband told me that her husband was acting the same way toward him as she did to me. I was quite surprised to learn that her husband acted the same toward my husband.

My husband and I tried to understand why they were acting hostile and giving us the cold shoulder for weeks. We talked about it because we were trying to figure out what we did wrong. We finally concluded that we did not do anything wrong, except they saw us as some sort of competition.

"Competitor of what?" we asked ourselves. We didn't understand why they saw us as competition, but one thing for sure, they clearly indicated to us that they did not want anything to do with us and didn't want us to acknowledge them at all while at church.

Anyway, one Sunday after service, we were heading back home. While driving home, we were talking about them not in a good way. We were irritated by this couple's behavior. We said to each other, "Who do they think they are?", "We didn't want anything from them", "How in the world could they acted like they didn't know us?", "How in the world could they treat any human being like this?", "Something must be wrong with them" and so on.

This had gone on for a few more Sundays. After the church service, we didn't talk about the service or the sermon, but somehow, they became our main subject until we arrived home. Then when we were at home, we completely forgot about them until the following Sunday.

This started to bother us. Talking about them not in good way did not make us feel good. We also knew, God was not pleased with us talking about them in the way we did. So, we decided to do something very different. We decided to treat them the way they treated us—ignoring them! Maybe, we thought, if we ignored them, we might not have any reason to talk about them and committing sin in the process.

As a matter of fact, I encouraged my husband to ignore her husband. "Don't acknowledge him. Since he treated you like a dirt bag, treat him the same way," and so on. We thought this was the perfect solution for us not sinning.

The following Sunday, as I walked in the church, I saw her sitting in same section, but I ignored her just as we said we would, but after the service, we still talked about them! Ignoring them didn't work! They still became our main subject, but this time, we talked as though we had some sort of victory.

I said to my husband, "Who do they think they are? They think they can blow us off like we are nobody. I can do the same thing too!

I showed them, and I'll show them even more," and so on. "Yes!" I felt like I had some sort of victory! I felt like, "Yes, I showed you." I was ready to do a victory lap around our house.

The following Sunday, as I walked into church, I was fully prepared to ignore her, and when I saw her, I pretended like I didn't see her. Then all of a sudden, from deep inside me, I heard, "Say hello to her," and I thought very briefly, *Why should I?* And I ignored that too.

Then immediately after service, we repeated the same things as the previous Sunday. We talked about them in bad way and as we had victory over them. The following Sunday came, I conducted myself the same as the previous Sunday. As I saw her seated around that same area again, I ignored her. Then I heard, "Go, say hello to her," but I ignored it again, thinking, *Why should I?*

After the service, I got into our car, and as I was putting on my seat belt, we were talking about them the same as the previous Sunday. Then I heard, "You did not worship me today." I knew this was God talking to me. I said to Him, "What do you mean? I just walked out of church!"

"I know you did! But you did not worship me today."

"What? What are you talking about God? I just walked out of church!"

Again, He said, "I know you did, but you still did not worship me." Then He said, "What did I say about worship? Did I not say, 'Obedience is better than sacrifice?'" (1 Samuel 15:22).

"Yes, but what didn't I obey you?"

Then He said, "Didn't I ask you to say 'hello' to her? You did not do what I asked you to do."

Then immediately, I said to Him, "How come you did not ask her to say 'hello' to me? You can ask her to do same thing!"

Then He said, "Do you think I didn't ask her to do the same thing to you?"

At that very moment, I was very surprised by His answer. I did not know God was asking her to do same thing! I thought, He only asked me to do such a thing. This revelation taught me something very new and important. Whenever two or more people are involved in a situation, He speaks to everyone who is involved. He asks everyone to do what is right. This was something I did not know until God revealed this to me.

He continued, "You got up early in the morning and spent two to three hours to prepare for the service. You didn't even have a decent meal because you needed to prepare your kids and yourself for the service. Then you went to church and clapped your hands, you sang, prayed, listen to the teaching, and gave an offering, but because of your disobedience, you failed to make your worship to be acceptable to me."

"My Scripture says"

> Therefore I urge you, brethren, by the mercies of God, to present your bodies a living and holy sacrifice, *acceptable to God*, which is your spiritual service of worship.
> (Romans 12:1, NASB)

> You also, as living stones, are being built up as a spiritual house for a holy priesthood, to offer up spiritual sacrifices *acceptable to God* through Jesus Christ.
> (1 Peter 2:5, NASB)

God was absolutely right about my worship. I did not worship Him with my spirit. I did not offer my spiritual sacrifice. I took so much time to prepare for the service, but my worship was not accepted by God. I just went to church to do what I normally did, just practicing my Sunday habit.

I realized God was not pleased with my ritual services. God was not looking for my routine attendance, but my obedience, my sincere worship. He wanted me to be a true worshipper. He wanted my obedience and respect for Him. I shared this with my husband what God had revealed to me. We realized how wrong we were.

Then God reminded me of these scriptures.

> Also if anyone competes as an athlete, he does not win the prize unless he competes according to the rules.
> (2 Timothy 2:5, NASB)

> Do you not know that those who run in a race all run, but only one receives the prize? Run in such a way that you may win.
> (1 Corinthians 9:24, NASB)

I realized she and I were in a race of obedience—the race set for her and me to say "hello". She and I were at the starting line of obedience with only one question to be answered, "Who is going to say 'hello' first?" I wanted to be the winner of this race by obeying God first. I wanted to make sure my worship was accepted by God.

I did not want to waste my worship. I didn't want my worship to be ruined by anyone else anymore. I was determined to make sure I reached the goal line first so I could win the prize. I wanted my worship to be accepted by God to win my prize. I wanted my prize!

The next Sunday, when I saw her, I walked up to her and said, "Hello," and gave her a big smile, then I walked to the pew where I always sit and sat down. She had a shocked and puzzled look on her face. Since I had not acknowledged her for weeks, she probably did not expect me to greet her.

From that Sunday, for several Sundays, I did the same thing over again. I acknowledged her every time I saw her. I did that to make sure my worship reached God.

It made me feel good to win the race of obedience. I knew my worship was accepted by God. My worship reached all the way up to God's heart. I knew God was very pleased with my obedience.

She began to acknowledge me just as I acknowledged her. We never became close friends, but at least, I didn't have any hard feelings toward her. And most importantly, God accepted my worship.

I didn't know what happened to her worship, their worships. Later, we found out they were in some kind of leadership position at that church. Perhaps, they acted that way toward us because they wanted us to treat them as superiors? I really don't know the real reason, but we knew, and the Lord knew, they ignored us intentionally.

However, when I learned that God asked her to do the same thing and she refused, I wondered about their future. At that time, I had this thought, *If she can't obey God for this simple thing, how can she obey God for something much bigger than this?* And I said to myself, "She won't obey God."

Then, I thought, *If she continually disobeys God like she was doing right now, I wonder how their life and future would turn out? I really wanted to see them many years later.* I didn't pray this to God, but I did want to see how the disobedient life would turn out.

Then twenty years later, through a mutual friend, we learned that they had been struggling with their life and with many things. Additionally, their marriage got destroyed and they divorced. I really didn't know the real reason why these things happened, and it made me feel sad for them, but I could only come to one conclusion—they may have lived a life of continually disobeying the Lord.

How About Your Worship?

Do you ever wonder about your worship? Is your worship accepted by God? I thought as long as I attended church services, my worship unto God was done for that day. Do you think like I did? If you attend church service, your worship is done. Do you do a similar thing like I did, ignoring someone intentionally?

Do you walk into His house of worship with anger, bitterness, resentment, or any other negative emotion, and do your best to avoid someone? How about when you go to work? Do you deliberately blow someone off because you got offended?

I believe most of us make a tremendous mistake in this area. We rather hold on to the offense than settle it before we worship God. Do you know what our Lord Jesus told us about this area?

> Therefore if you bring your gift to the altar, and there remember that your brother has something against you, leave your gift there before the altar, and go your way. First be reconciled to your brother, and then come and offer your gift.
> (Matthew 5:23–24, NKJV)

We are supposed to reconcile any issue(s) before we worship God. But we rather hold on to the offenses. We rather wait for others to make the first move, or we rather ignore the issues all together, or we rather pretend there is no issue at all. We think if we ignore it, then it will go away, like I did, but that's not true. For instance, if you think about the person, or the incident, and then you get angry, then that is a clear sign that you are still harboring the offense in your heart.

Go settle the issue. Don't wait for others to make the first move. You make the first move for your worship and for your prize! Jesus says that "you" go and settle the issues and then come to the altar to worship. This is true worship!

You may want to say you didn't do anything wrong. Therefore, you don't need to settle any issues because others did all the wrong. You may be right! You may not have started the argument, or the issue, but if you harbor anger and treat others with negative emotion, you are also doing wrong.

You read my story, we didn't do any wrong to that couple either. God knows our heart. We just wanted to acknowledge them and greet them, that was all, but they deliberately, intentionally, and purposefully blew us off. But when we decided to treat them the same way they treated us, that made us wrong because we repaid them evil with evil.

> "Do not repay anyone evil for evil. Be careful to do what is right in the eyes of everyone. If it is possible, as far as it depends on you, live at peace with everyone."
> (Romans 12:17–18, NIV)

You heard the phrase use by nonbelievers, "Two wrong don't make a right". You know this definition. It is not acceptable to do something bad to someone just because they did something bad to you. Although non-Christians don't know God, they know this is wrong to practice. But many believers—followers of Christ—practice repaying evil for evil without a second thought.

"If it is possible, as far as it depends on you, live at peace with everyone." It doesn't matter who they are, believers or nonbelievers, you own up to what you did wrong regardless of who started the argument or issue, or how it got started, and what got started. Regardless of how many times you curse, how long you got upset, or how many words you've said wrong. What matters is, are you owning up to your mistake? Don't focus on the mistakes of others.

God wants you to own up to all your intentions and purposes. That's what matters to God. Make it right before God, you have an obligation to make it right before you come to God to worship. As long as it depends on you, as a Christian, fulfill the obligation to the Father and to others. Do all you can do to live in peace with everyone." This is the true spiritual sacrifice of worship acceptable to God.

> "Trust in the Lord, and do good; Dwell in the land, and feed on His faithfulness."
> (Psalm 37:3, NKJV)

> "Therefore, to one who knows the right thing to do and does not do it, to him it is sin."
> (James 4:17, NASB)

If you know what right thing to do, but do not do it, it is a sin. Compete according to the rules. "Obedience is better than sacrifice." You obey His Word. You are in the race for obedience. Obey God for your prize. You are not obeying God for someone else's prize. You! Run your race of obedience to win your prize. Run your race for your worship and for your peaceful relationship with God and for your blessing.

Don't allow anything or anyone to ruin your relationship with the Lord. Nothing is worthier and more important than your relationship with God. God is the source of your life. Don't let Satan take advantage of you, your worship, your relationship with God, and your blessings. Whatever it is or whomever it is, they are not that important to ruin your worship and your sincere relationship with God. It is not worth it!

> If you forgive anyone, I do too. For what I have forgiven—if I have forgiven anything—it is for you in the presence of Christ. I have done this so that we may not be taken advantage of by Satan. For we are not ignorant of his schemes.
> (2 Corinthians 2:10–11, HCSB)

Trust in His justice. He knows all truth. If God sees they deserve His justice, He will make it right for you. In due season, He will let others know what they did wrong and how they did wrong. But in the meantime, you do what is right. Don't worry about how others might think of you or what they may say about you. The only thing you need to be concerned about is how God thinks about you and what God says about you.

> If your enemy is hungry, give him food to eat; And if he is thirsty, give him water to drink; For you will heap burning coals on his head, And the Lord will reward you.
> (Proverbs 25:21–22, NASB)

> It may be that the Lord will look on my affliction, and that the *Lord will repay* me with good for his cursing this day.
> (2 Samuel 16:12, NKJV)

We are all in a race of obedience. Obey God for your true worship and for your blessing. You'll see His glory.

Do you not know that those who run in a race all run, but only one receives the prize? Run in such a way that you may win.
(1 Corinthians 9:24, NASB)

But Samuel replied, "What is more pleasing to the Lord: your burnt offerings and sacrifices or your obedience to his voice? Listen! Obedience is better than sacrifice, and submission is better than offering the fat of rams."
(1 Samuel 15:22, NLT)

As God is alive, His word is alive. And His "Word" will prove to you, He is alive.

5

Unhappy with God: Numbers of Hair on My Head

When we moved to Killeen, Texas, we purchased a house and, in the process, acquired extra expenses each month. I wanted to work to help support my husband so we could have a nice house. We didn't suffer for lack of finances, we just had a little more expense than what we were accustomed to, and it made me feel a little uneasy. This was my reason for wanting to work as I believed the extra income would be helpful to us.

I considered a few options for work, but there weren't that many choices. Working outside of the house was not a better choice as it presented some challenges. Our children at the time were still young and needed to go to daycare while I worked. After I calculated the cost of daycare, most of money I would earn would go to pay for daycare.

So, I found work as a seamstress that I could do at home. Sewing was the perfect type of work for me. I could control my own hours and the amount of work that I would do. More importantly, our children didn't have to go to daycare.

I knew very little about sewing, but I met someone from the church to help me. As I started to work, I brought the amount of work home that I thought I could handle to finish within the deadline.

Although I controlled the quantity of work, I often found myself working past midnight—until two, three, or four in the morning. It took me more time to finish than I expected. Sometimes, it took all night to finish it, either because I had to take care of things that day, or because I made mistakes and needed to redo the entire sewing. It began to overwhelm me, and I was very unhappy with my circumstance.

Sewing took so much time away from me to get the proper rest I needed, and it also took too much time away from me reading my Bible and praying. Whenever I prayed or read my Bible, I rushed through it because I needed to sew.

A discontented feeling started to rise up within me. I began to have unhealthy thoughts toward God. "As He said He would look after me, He is not looking out for me. We need more financial increase but there was no chance at this moment."

You see, my husband was in the military at that time; therefore, our financial increase could only come through his promotion, and there was no promotion due anytime soon. Therefore, if we wanted financial increase, I needed to work.

More Feelings of Discontentment

As the days went by, more often, further complaining thoughts came into my mind. I was in a serious spiritual battle. One moment, I said to myself, "I should not meditate on these thoughts". Then another moment, I noodled on ungrateful thoughts like, "Well, I gave my tithe and offerings, sent funds to mission field, and gave time to church but where is our increase, where is our blessing?"

"If we did not give all those monies to the church, we probably would have more money right now, and perhaps, I would not have to sew to earn money", "I am working hard and stressing out because of money, but where is God's promise? Where is the increase that He promised?"

"If we are going to have any increase, how will this happen?", "Is God really going to look out for us?", "If He will look out for us, when will this happen? And how is He going to do it?" etc. As a side note, God did way more than enough for our life! I will share it with you in a later story.

Although I had all these ungrateful thoughts, I tried to resist them. I tried to think positive thoughts, and I tried to replace those negative thoughts with grateful ones. I fought my own thoughts by saying to myself, "How in the world can I even think like this? After all, God saved me from eternal hell. I need to be grateful to Him. I must thank God for healing my husband from chronic asthma. I must thank God for all the good He did for us, our health, this house, car, our children's safety and so forth. I am not supposed to have these ungrateful thoughts."

"Though God may not give me more money, I have eternal salvation. Eternal salvation alone is a very grateful thing! How dare I even think about being ungrateful? I am not supposed to think like this." I really tried to resist all the negative thoughts by self-reproach by thinking about all the positive thoughts, but immediately, negative thoughts seized me again. I tried to shake it off, but very often, I found myself in the middle of all kinds of resentful thoughts.

Number of Hair

In the midst of this huge spiritual battle and all the sewing that I needed to do, I still made sure I took time to pray and read my Bible. Though, I could not spend as much time as I wanted, I still found time to pray and read my Bible. One evening, after I had finished sewing, I grabbed my Bible to read. As I sat down to open the Bible, God asked me a question, "How do you understand this scripture,

'But the very hairs of your head are all numbered?'
(Matthew 10:30, NKJV)

I answered Him, "Well? It means, you know everything about me?" He then said, "You are right. If you know, I know everything about you, do you think that I also know all of your thoughts?" I instantly knew what exact thoughts He's talking about.

At that moment, I immediately felt so embarrassed for having resentful thoughts toward God. It made me feel like I got caught stealing right there and then! Then I said to Him, "If you know all my thoughts, why do you have to ask me about this? Why do you need to hear it from me? Why couldn't you let it go? Don't you know, this is embarrassing to me?"

Then He said, "Let me ask you a question, if you knew which child did something wrong, then why do you ask them who did it? Why couldn't you let it go? Why do you need to hear this from him? Why couldn't you let it go without asking? You already know who did it."

I answered, "Well, I ask because I do not want him to hide it from me. I want him to be honest with me. If he admits it to me, he is acknowledging his wrong and acknowledging me. By admitting it to me, he provides an opportunity for me to teach him about wrong and right."

Then God said, "That is the exact thing I desire from you! Though I know all your thoughts and mistakes, I wish to hear from you. If you admit it to me, you are acknowledging me! And acknowledging your mistake. By admitting it to me, you give me the opportunity to minister to you. Although I know all your thoughts, I want you to admit it to me. If you hold it from me, I can't minister to you. If you try to hide it from me, you are not giving me an opportunity to minister to you."

You probably understood what God was saying to me, but I will give you an example. If you knew which child did wrong and you ask that very child, "Hey, John, did you do this? If he says, no, you cannot minister to him until he admits his wrongdoing. If that child continually denies his action and tries to hide from you, you can't minister to him. You may spank him for lying, but you can't minister to him in his heart."

Wow! How awesome our Father is? Once and for all, I realized, I can't hide anything from God. He knew all my thoughts. I prayed to God every day, but I never mentioned to God my discontentment. I was too embarrassed to mention this to God and a bit scared to have these kinds of resentful thoughts. I thought, if I tried shaking negative thoughts off, it would eventually go away.

I didn't know, I could talk to Him honestly about my discontentment. I thought, I could only talk to God about my needs and my problems, but I didn't know I could talk to Him about my displeasure thinking toward Him.

Inner Room

With this communication, God gave me a huge revelation that I *"can"* let God know about all my thoughts—good or bad. Because He knows all my thoughts before I even mention them to Him.

Let's look at some scriptures.

> Behind the second curtain was a room called the Most Holy Place… But only the high priest entered the inner room, and that only once a year, and never without blood, which he offered for himself and for the sins the people had committed in ignorance.
> (Hebrews 9:3, 7; NIV)

> Therefore, brothers and sisters, since we have confidence to enter the *Most Holy Place (inner room)* by the blood of Jesus, by a new and living way opened for us through the curtain, that is, his body.
> (Hebrews 10:19–20, NIV)

> But you, when you pray, go into *your inner room*, close your door and pray to your Father who is *in secret*, and your Father who sees what is done in secret will reward you.
>
> (Matthew 6:6, NASB)

Jesus is not only talking about the physical location of the inner room which means nothing to God. Jesus is talking more about the spiritual inner room of your heart. With the blood of Jesus, you enter the Most Holy Place called the Inner Room, which was impossible to access in the time of the Old Testament.

Only the high priest went in and only once a year, but by the blood of Jesus, God invites you and me into the most secret place—the "Inner Room" of intimacy. He invites you into His deepest parts of this secret place to commune. Therefore, you also need to invite God into the deepest part of your heart.

You can't have an authentic relationship with God if you keep secrets from Him, which, by the way, God knows it anyway. Just as you can't have a real relationship with your spouse who keeps secrets from you, you can't have a truthful relation with someone who is untruthful.

No one can have a sincere relationship with anyone who is dishonest. The same holds true with our relationship with God, who dwell in the Secret place, we must approach Him with an honest and truthful heart. And God who dwells in the secret place can only be found by a person with an honest and truthful heart.

> If I regard iniquity (secret) in my heart, The Lord will not hear. But certainly God has heard me He has attended to the voice of my prayer.
>
> (Psalm 66:18–19, NKJV)

> But your iniquities (secret) have separated you from your God; And your sins have hidden His face from you, So that He will not hear.
>
> (Isaiah 59:2, NKJV)

If you keep secrets, it only keeps you in captive. You might think you are actually keeping secrets from God, but everything is known to God including your secrets. Only you are the one locked up in captivity by your own secrets. Secret keeps you in imprisoned. You become a prisoner of your own secrets. God wants us to enjoy total freedom. He wants you to experience complete freedom not partial freedom. He wants you to be free from all the burdens you've carried for a long time. He knows it all!

When God ask me that question and revealed Matthew 6:6 to me, I learned how to pray honestly. I didn't know I could be totally honest with God. Whenever I prayed, I never mention to Him any of my discontentment (It was my secret). I tried to get rid of all the ungrateful thoughts before I prayed.

But since I learned, He knows all my thoughts and intentions, I just let God know everything. My angers, concerns, worries, disappointments, shame, resentment toward God or to men, and whatever it is. I learned, I need to invite God into the deepest part of my heart just as He let me into the "Most Holy Place" of His.

What Is in Your Heart?

What secret is in the center of your heart? Whatever is considered a secret to you, it is not a secret to Him at all. He knows it all. Just as, He knows the number of hairs on your head. Nothing is hidden from God. Your pains, your disgrace, addictions, eating disorders, anger at God, discontentment, hatred toward someone, whatever the secret it is, God knows all.

> And there is no creature hidden from His sight,
> but all things are naked and open to the eyes of
> Him to whom we must give account.
> (Hebrews 4:13, NKJV)

> Would not God search this out? For He knows the secrets of the heart.
>
> (Psalm 44:21, NKJV)

God knows all about you and everything about you, all your thoughts, words, actions, etc. To God, nothing is a secret. He just wants you to be honest with Him. I encourage you to be honest with God. When you pray, pray to God in truth. Tell God, what you think you can't tell anyone else. He is waiting for you to be honest with Him. He knows all.

He just wants you to admit and be completely honest with Him. Your confession of whatever secret is your acknowledgement that God knows all. The confession of your secrets is your confession of wanting to have a true honest relationship with God.

Pour out your heart. Tell Him! He already knows all. Just tell Him everything. Give God an opportunity to minister to you. Let God reveal to you how much he loves you and that how much He is longing for you. He will not embarrass you. He will cover you with His love.

> "Trust in Him at all times, you people; *Pour out your heart* before Him; God is a refuge for us Selah."
>
> (Psalm 62:8, NKJV)

Don't let Satan to deceive you. He is the father of liars!

> "Whenever he speaks a lie, he speaks from his own nature, for he is a liar and the father of lies."
>
> (John. 8:44, NASB)

Remember, the devil will try to prevent you from being truthful to God. The devil will try to prevent you from becoming totally free. The devil will lie to you by saying, "God is going to hold this against you, letting God know will not do you any good, God doesn't care for you, or it is too shameful to let God know about these things". Don't let the devil lie to you. God knows all about you.

Before I realized I could be truthful with God, the devil had a good hold of me for quite some time. I felt so ashamed of myself in having ungrateful thoughts toward God. Though I felt guilty and ashamed about myself, but whenever negative thoughts came to my mind, I still pondered on it, which eventually would have separated me from God. But through God's grace, I was totally set free from this severe spiritual battle when I became totally honest with God.

Meaningless Repetition

> "And when you are praying, do not use meaningless repetition as the Gentiles do, for they suppose that they will be heard for their many words."
> (Matthew 6:7, NASB)

First, when you talk honestly, you can't make meaningless repetition. How can anyone speak like that? If you speak truthfully to anyone, you can't speak vain repetition at the same time. It is very hard to do. Honest talk is straight forward talk, you talk about what's in your heart. Vain repetition is done when a person doesn't speak truthful and not from the heart. Speak truthfully to God then you won't speak meaningless repetition.

God will not be moved by meaningless repetition. God pays attention to your prayer only if you speak truthfully to Him. And if your prayer is heard by God, you will also receive an answer from God.

Some people acknowledge God knows everything but at the same time, they try to hide the truth from Him. They draw near to God physically, but their heart does not draw near to God. Draw your heart near to Him. He will draw His heart close to you also.

> "These people draw near to Me with their mouth, And honor Me with their lips, But their heart is far from Me."
>
> (Matthew 15:8, NKJV)

Don't go through an unnecessary spiritual battle like I did. Only honest prayer moves God! He is your exceedingly great rewarder! All the things you have been praying for, He will reward you openly and honorably. He will reward you over and above and beyond all your imaginations and thoughts before the whole world, before angels and men, and even before your adversaries. Speak to God honestly from the deepest parts of your heart. Your rewards will be great! Draw your heart close to God.

> Do not fear, for you will not be ashamed; Neither be disgraced, for you will not be put to shame; For you will forget the shame of your youth And will not remember the reproach of your widowhood anymore.
>
> (Isaiah 54:4, NKJV)

> Instead of your shame you shall have double honor, And instead of confusion they shall rejoice in their portion. Therefore, in their land they shall possess double; Everlasting joy shall be theirs.
>
> (Isaiah 61:7, NKJV)

As God is alive, His word is alive. And His "Word" will prove to you, He is alive.

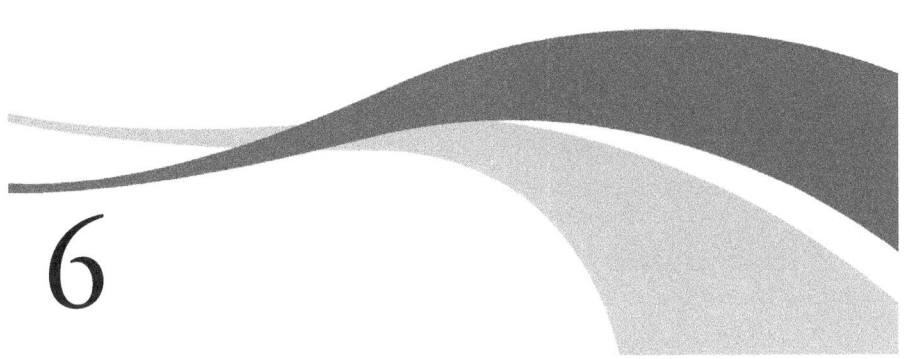

6

Bug Story 1: God Saved the Drowning Bug

One summer morning while living in Texas, I stepped out into my backyard. There on the patio we had a small children's pool—one I had purchased from Walmart. It was made of plastic and its size was about five feet in diameter. Its depth was about a foot and a half and water was still in it from the day before. When I looked inside the pool, a bunch of tiny bugs were floating around in the water. The size of these bugs was almost the same size as a lady bug and their color was a golden brown.

Many of the bugs were already dead, but there were three or four bugs that were still alive. One of them was very much alive, and this one caught my attention. This particular bug may have entered the water not too long ago. It had a lot of strength left. It swam strong in the water attempting to get to the side of the pool. When it finally reached the side of the pool, it tried very hard to climb up on the wall of the pool to escape the water, but it couldn't because the wall was too slippery.

Then all of a sudden, the Spirit of the Lord spoke to me, "Imaging that bug is you."

Huh? That bug is me? As I was observing the bug as myself, thoughts were running through my mind. *What if I'm floating like this bug in the Pacific Ocean?* I mentioned earlier the bug size was like a lady bug, and the pool was about five feet in diameter. To this bug, that pool was like the Pacific Ocean. Nothing was there to help it out!

I was imagining myself floating in the ocean. "I am floating in the Pacific Ocean like this bug is floating in this pool. There is no ship passing by, and there is no one to help me out. If no help comes to me as soon as possible, I will die." My life is in a devastating and fearsome situation. Like that tiny bug, my destiny was guaranteed to die. I cannot see any hope. There is no way out. My final fate is death for sure!

As I continually observed the bug as me, it swam across the water to reach the side of the pool and tried to climb up the wall to escape, but it failed. Then it rested to regain its strength. While it was resting for new strength, a light wind pushed the bug farther away from the wall. The wind pushed it into the center of the pool, so it had to swim a long distant to get to the wall. When it reached the wall, it tried so hard to get out of the pool but again it failed.

This had happened three times. Then suddenly, the Spirit of Lord asked me to pretend like I am God. "I am God? I am God!" I am looking down on the bug like God is looking down on me. When I compared myself to that bug, I was like mighty giant to that bug! Then the Spirit of the Lord asked, "If you are God, what can you do to help it out?"

I immediately answered to God, "It is easy, God. I can lift up the pool to get all the water out or I can scoop it out with my hand." Then He said to me, "Scoop it out with your hand." So, I made my hand as a cup and scooped it out.

Then the water in my hand ran through my fingers, and now this tiny bug was in my hand, and I tossed it out in the air. As I tossed it out in the air, it started to flap its wings like dancing in the air. Every time it flapped its wings, it seemed to say, "I'm alive, *flap, flap, flap,* I'm alive, *flap, flap, flap,* I'm alive, *flap, flap, flap,*" and it flew away.

I began to have a deep thought within me. "What caused those bugs to jump into the water? What was tempting them? Is it the moonlight that reflected on the water? What was it? Whatever it was, many bugs were tempted to their death. Whatever it was, all the bugs paid the consequence of temptation, except only the one rescued by God.

The Spirit of God said to me, "Like that bug, in your life, you may fall into the same situation, but I will be there to rescue you, just as you rescued that bug. It doesn't matter where you are, I will be with you always to help you." As I scoop that bug out of death, He promised me that He will scoop me out of death.

When God spoke this to me, I received absolute assurance He will always be there to help me. I may be in a far worst situation than that bug, but God will save me just as He saved this tiny bug. He will scoop me out of every dangerous situation.

When I rescued that bug, it was so effortless for me to do. To that bug, it couldn't do anything to save its life. But for me, it was so easy to save that bug. I just had to bend over to scoop it out. I may put myself in dangerous situation in the future like this bug did, but God will be there to save me because it is absolutely effortless for Him to do it.

Then all of sudden, a song from a chorus rose up inside of me, and I began to praise the Father.

The song title is, "My Soul in Sad Exile" from an old Hymnal. The chorus goes like this:

> "I've anchored my soul in the haven of rest, I'll sail the wide seas no more. The tempest may sweep o'er the wild stormy deep; in Jesus, I'm safe ever more"

Imaging yourself drowning in the Pacific Ocean because of the mistakes you made, and no one is near to save you. Some of you may be in that situation right now, like that bug. What caused you to be in that situation? What was tempting you? How did you think it was going to benefit you? Are you feeling like there's no way out, like that bug? Don't you know that your Heavenly Father wants to rescue you just as He rescued that bug? Didn't God say He can do anything?

There is nothing impossible for God to rescue you. Can you believe Him that he can do anything for you? You do know our loving Father wants to help you. Whatever the reason you got into trouble, God is, right now, there to rescue you. It is so effortless for Him to do this. God's mighty hand will scoop you out of the ocean just like he did for this tiny bug.

> Consider the ravens, for they neither sow nor reap; they have no storeroom nor barn, and yet God feeds them; how much more valuable you are than the birds!... Consider the lilies, how they grow: they neither toil nor spin; but I tell you, not even Solomon in all his glory clothed himself like one of these.
> (Luke 12:24, 27; NASB)

If God cares so much for ravens and the lilies of the field, how much more will He care for you? If God pays this much attention to a tiny bug, how much more is He paying attention to you? When Jesus came on earth to die, He did not die for those ravens, lilies, or that bug. He died for you and me! He purchased you with His precious blood. He did not purchase ravens, lilies, or that bug with His blood. If He purchased you with His precious blood, how important are you to God?

You are very and particularly important to God! You must know this for sure otherwise the devil will try to confuse you. This is especially true when you are in a bad situation, the devil will try to lead you to believe that God doesn't care for you. But He promised, He would never leave you or forsake you. He is always with you to protect you, guide you, and rescue you (John 14:18).

Be strong and courageous. Do not be afraid or terrified because of them, for the Lord your God goes with you; he will never leave you nor forsake you.
(Deuteronomy 31:6, NIV)

And I will ask the Father, and He will give you another Counselor to be with you forever.
(John 14:16, HCSB)

He only is my rock and my salvation; He is my defense; I shall not be moved.
(Psalm 62:6, NKJV)

Now I know that the Lord saves His anointed; He will answer him from His holy heaven with the saving strength of His right hand.
(Psalm 20:6, NKJV)

Do not fear, do not worry, because He loves you dearly. He will help you just as He helped that bug. You are more important than a bug. Amen.

Let Me Pray for You

"Father God, I pray in the name of Jesus, I don't know the person who is reading this story right now. But if this person needs help from you like that tiny bug, help this person right now. Father, send help to this person to save them, just as you sent help to save that tiny bug. In Jesus name I pray, amen."

Just in case you are not a Christian, you must first accept Jesus Christ as your Lord and Savior before you can ask God for help. You need to invite Jesus into your heart to make Jesus Lord of your life. Would you open your heart and invite Jesus into your life now? Please repeat this prayer:

> Dear Jesus,
> I am a sinner.
>> I repent of my sins.
>> Please forgive me and save me by your shed blood;
>> Come into my life, I receive your gift of forgiveness.
>> I open my heart to receive Jesus as my own personal Lord and Savior.
>> In Jesus name I pray, amen.

If you said this prayer, plant yourself into a local church to grow in Christ and to develop a relationship with follow Christians. This is very important for your spiritual growth and walk with Jesus. Learn to trust in the Lord, He will never fail you. Amen.

As God is alive, His word is alive. And His "Word" will prove to you, He is alive.

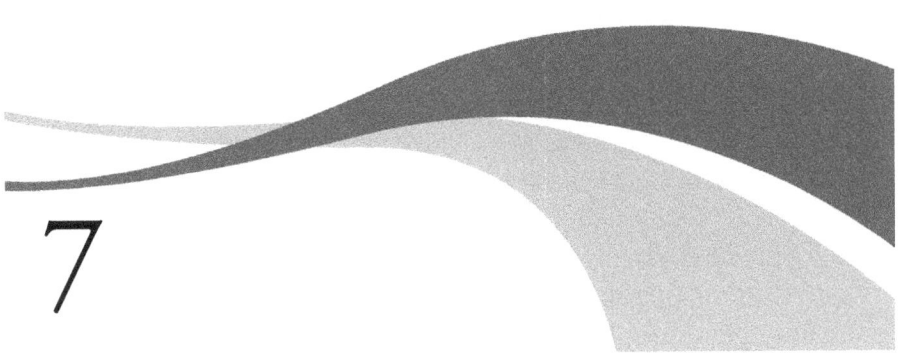

7

Bug Story 2: Bug Gives Testimony

God revealed an amazing truth to me through this wonderful experience of a simple bug. God showed me that in a bug's realm, bugs do not understand the human realm. They can't even comprehend that we are living on the same planet. We know that bugs exist, and we see them all the time, but bugs do not know us.

But what if the bug I rescued went back to its community and family to share its experience. Do you believe its community and family would believe that bug's story? Would they believe the story of how it almost died, but God miraculously save it through my hand?

It might share this amazing story with other bugs with so much excitement like, "Do you know what happened to me? I was drowning in this huge ocean with no hope, and there was no ship passing by. There was no island close by that I could swim to save myself but a hand! An amazing hand came down from above, and, out of nowhere, scooped me up out of death! All the bugs around me had drowned, but I was saved by the hand! I know for sure that something much bigger than us is living on this planet!"

So, how do you think the other bugs would respond? Would they have responded with excitement? Would they acknowledge mankind through its testimony? What do you think? Do you believe they would believe this bug's testimony? Probably not! No bug would have believed it! Even though what the bug told them was absolutely true, they wouldn't believe it because bugs can't understand the realm of man.

So, what's the problem with this bug's family and community? The problem is that they only acknowledge and understand their realm—the realm of bugs! Perhaps only the realm of insects! They only understand their world, concepts, and rules. They only understand their experience and the knowledge they have.

Although bugs cannot understand and see man's realm, it doesn't mean we are not here, right? We are living right here with them. We are here and live very close to them, and yet they still don't understand our realm, or the realms of any other creature for that matter. When we get close to it, it senses something is getting closer, so it flies away, but it doesn't have the capability to understand or acknowledge the realm of mankind, what we are, and who we are.

> But God gives it a body as he has determined, and to each kind of seed he gives its own body. Not all flesh is the same: People have one kind of flesh, animals have another, birds another and fish another. There are also heavenly bodies and there are earthly bodies; but the splendor of the heavenly bodies is one kind, and the splendor of the earthly bodies is another. The sun has one kind of splendor, the moon another and the stars another; and star differs from star in splendor.
> (1 Corinthians 15:38–41, NIV)

We can look at this scripture in this way. God made the realms as he has determined (Genesis 1–2). Man's realm, animal's realm, bird's realm, fish's realm, heavenly realm (spiritual realm), earthly realm (natural realm), and realms of the galaxy. Have you ever thought about the realm of the ocean?

Let's think about it for little a bit. Any creature living in the ocean doesn't understand the realm of land or the realm of the sky.

Creatures in the oceans only understand the realm of the ocean; they only understand the things of the oceans.

You do know that seals and sea lions hunt for their food in the ocean, but they spend a great deal of time on land resting and raising their young. On a very small scale, they know the realms of the ocean and land.

So, let's just say they go to the depth in the ocean to share the story of what they saw and experience on the land. "Hey, do you know there's another realm beside the ocean? It has mountains, rocks, sand, trees, flowers, and we can see the sky, and we can see birds flying over our heads. It is all very beautiful and wonderful."

Do you think the other ocean creatures would believe their testimony? Even though what the seals and sea lions told them is absolutely true, the majority of fishes would think seals and sea lions are crazy and won't believe their story because fishes can't comprehend the realms of land and sky even exist.

What about the whale? This magnificent creature lives 100 percent of the time in the realm of ocean, but it hunts its food not only in the ocean but also on the coastline. Some whales know not only the realm of the ocean but also the realm of land where it too hunts for its food.

Then let's say the whale goes to its friends to share what it knows. "Hey, do you know there is a realm of land above the ocean? Sometimes, I go there to hunt for my food. The land is so amazing and beautiful. I saw trees, flowers, the blue sky, and I saw birds flying over my head in the sky too."

Do you think that the other fishes would believe this testimony? Probably not! And they might even say to the whale, "You are crazy. There are no other realms another than this ocean we live in!" Because they can't understand the realm of land by its experiences, concept, knowledge, and rules, they reject all the truth about the realms of land and sky.

The same holds true about the human realm. So many people only understand the realm of the earth, the realm of nature, but fail to understand the realm of the spirit, the realm of God. God is absolutely real, just like you are real, and God is remarkably closer to you than you think, but people deny God because they cannot see God with their natural eye.

People are so accustomed to accepting and believing only what they can see, hear, feel, touch, taste, and smell, and because most people have not experience God's miracles in their lives, they do not accept the testimony of others, just like the bugs and the fishes.

Men are accustomed to only accept and believe what they can understand—the natural realm of concepts, its rules, education, and experiences—and they deny all spiritual things because they cannot comprehend the realm of spirit with their natural mind and senses.

Let us give a little more thought to the topic so we gain a better understanding. Let's go back to the time when there was no electricity, television, telephone, and the internet. Do you recall from early history books that sixteenth century people believed the earth was flat?

People back then also only understood things they could see with their natural eye. They only comprehended and accepted what they saw, heard, touched, tasted, and smelled as they were limited in understanding and depending on their five senses.

Anything beyond this was all a guessing game to them, until facts were presented, and then they could have accepted it. Most people died at that time believing the earth was flat, but the fact of the matter is the earth is round as proven by Ferdinand Magellan. The same holds true for the spiritual realm. Because they can't understand it based on the natural realm of concepts, ideas, and experiences, they simply dismiss and deny the spiritual realm and God.

Let me give you one more example to help drive the point home. A long time ago, my ancestors in South Korea didn't believe other human races and cultures could have existed on the other side of the earth. They thought that there were no other humans living on the same planet as themselves. They only understood the realm of their family, tribe, community, and perhaps, very close neighboring countries like Japan or China.

They heard, occasionally, there are other humans like us living in another part of earth. They heard these people have blue eyes, blonde hair, white skin, curry hair, dark skin, but because they never saw another human living on the same planet, most people rejected what they heard and considered this folklore.

Most people said, "I am not going to believe this until I see one of these humans." All those people who did not believe the truth are no longer here with us, and the ones who didn't accept the story were proved to be very wrong.

That's what most people say about Jesus. Jesus lives in the spiritual realm and came into the natural realm to tell us about the spiritual realm. He came to let us know the spiritual realm is absolutely real!

Jesus also sent Paul, Peter, John, James, and many others modern-day prophets, and me, to tell you about the spiritual realm. I do not know about the spiritual realm as much as Jesus knows, but on a small scale, God has revealed so much of the spiritual realm to me, so I can share with you that God is real, and His realm is indeed real.

I have never seen God with my naked eye, but I decided to accept the testimonies of others, "That God is real, and He remembered all your sins." I read and read His Word to find out about Him, and through the grace of God, I met God and saw God through my spiritual eyes. You may not know God, but if I say to you "He is not real", then I am absolutely lying to you at this very moment because God is absolutely real.

> For ever since the world was created, people have seen the earth and sky. Through everything God made, they can clearly see his invisible qualities—his eternal power and divine nature. So, they have no excuse for not knowing God.
> (Romans 1:20, NLT)

Look around you. He has given us so much evidence of His existence through all of His creations. His creations are everywhere for us to see and enjoy but because you cannot see God, you accept other information—false information about His creation.

Don't reject God because you cannot see the spiritual realm with natural eyes. Just because you can't see God with your natural eyes does not mean He is not real. Don't deny the spiritual realm and God because you can't comprehend with your natural mind. Just because you can't see doesn't mean it does not exist. Just as most fishes cannot see, nor comprehend the realm of land or sky, does not mean we and the land don't exist.

How wonderful and what great blessing and benefit it is to those who belong to Him and understand that God is very real.

Many other bugs couldn't understand that humans are real, but that bug I saved clearly understood humans are real and that its life was rescued by a human. Even though many bugs didn't believe it, that bug knew for sure God saved its life through my hand. Read God's Word. Allow God to reveal His realm to you. He will gladly reveal it to you, and it brings Him great pleasure in doing so.

> You will seek Me and find Me when you search for Me with all your heart.
> (Jeremiah 29:13, NASB)

> Draw near to God and He will draw near to you. Cleanse your hands, you sinners; and purify your hearts, you double-minded.
> (James 4:8, NKJV)

It is not difficult at all if you truly seek Him. As God knows and sees your heart that you desire to know Him, He will reveal Himself to you more quickly than you could think. Draw close to him by reading His Word and attending His church services. God will draw close to you very swiftly than you could imagine. Don't be double-minded. Set your mind and heart in getting to know God.

Don't let the god of this world (Satan) to deceive you in thinking and believing there is no spiritual realm and that there is no God.

> *"For the message of the cross is foolishness to those who are perishing,* but to us who are being saved it is the power of God."
> (1 Corinthians 1:18, NKJV)

Are you the perishing one? Only to those who are perishing "the message of the cross is foolishness." Just like that bug I saved experienced, its message to the other bugs may have seemed very foolish to them.

Of course, the message of God is foolish to so many people because they cannot and will not be able to be comprehended with man's natural mind, or with the realm of man's knowledge. It can only be comprehended by the renewed mind and the spiritual mind.

And God clearly explains why the message of God is foolish to perishing people.

> Satan, who is the god of this world, *has blinded the minds of those who don't believe.* They are unable to see the glorious light of the Good News. They don't understand this message about the glory of Christ, who is the exact likeness of God.
> (2 Corinthians 4:4, NLT)

Don't let Satan blind your mind anymore. Open your heart and mind to God's invitation. Until you decide to open yourself to God's invitation, you cannot see His glory for your life because the spiritual realm of things can only be understood by the spiritual mind.

Let's invite Jesus Christ into your life. Once you make Him your Lord and Savior, He will take care of you just as He took care of that tiny bug. He knows everything about you and all about you; therefore, He knows how to help you.

Please repeat this prayer:

> Dear Jesus, I am a sinner.
> I repent of my sins.
> > Please forgive me and save me by your shed blood;
> > Come into my life, I receive your gift of forgiveness.

IS GOD REALLY ALIVE? BY AE CHA ARROYO

I open my heart to receive Jesus as my own personal Lord and Savior.
In Jesus name I pray, amen.

May God richly bless you as you decide to walk with Him.

As God is alive, His word is alive. And His "Word" will prove to you, He is alive.

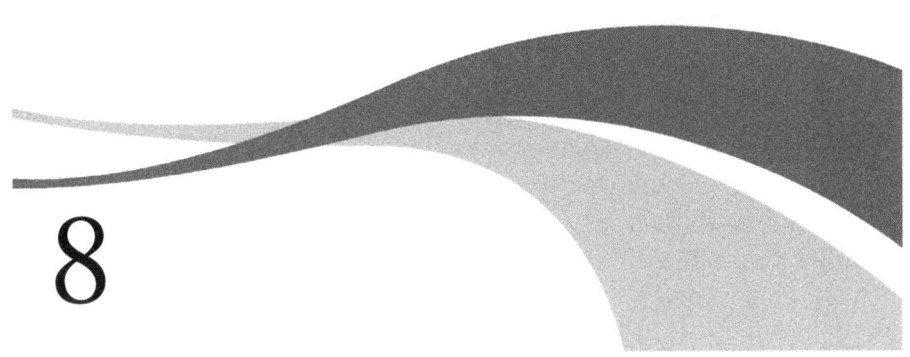

8

Selling Our House: How Did I Teach You?

This testimony happened to us when we were ready to move from Killeen, Texas, to Seattle, Washington. We were living in our first brand-new house for about two and half years. Then my husband, who was in the military, received orders to relocate to Seattle, Washington.

We knew when we bought our house, we might be asked once more to relocate by the government. We were hoping to avoid a new assignment. We thought that this might work out for us because my husband had only a few more years left to retire after twenty years of service.

Well, what we had hoped for didn't happen. My husband received a new assignment, and we had to relocate. Now, we were facing a huge problem. We needed to sell the house in an extremely difficult market. The next day, we spoke with a real estate agent, and the agent told us what we already suspected. This was a buyer market.

The market was extremely bad for anyone needing to sell a home. We were also told that it might take a very long time to sell. The agent was right about this because even within our own community, many homes had been listed for sale for many months. Some homes in our neighborhood had been empty for a long time, and many sellers were struggling to find buyers.

An agent suggested to us since we did not own the house for a long time to build any equity; it might be better for us to rent it rather than selling. Well, we didn't want to rent. We wanted to sell. He said he would try to sell it for us, but it would be very difficult.

Then he suggested to us, it might be a little easier for him if we sell the house at the price we bought it for, and pay the agency fee from our own pocket. We did not like either of his suggestions—renting or paying the agency fee from our own money. We were stuck between a rock and a hard place.

The only and the best option we had was to pray to God. We started praying to God, and at the same time, we also took pictures of our house and posted it anywhere we could to find a buyer. I asked God to sell our house for us. I told God, according to His Word, He knew, before we knew, we needed to move. Since He knows everything, He also knew we needed to sell our house too.

I asked God to bring someone to buy our house. I let God know, we do not wish to spend any more money into the house. We invested quite of money on the house because it was brand-new. We had put in grass, garden, fence, window blinds curtains, and so forth.

Praying for Selling our House

I said, "Father, we cannot afford to spend any more money on this house. As you know, we invested a lot of money. We want to use an agency to help us sell this house, but if we use a real estate agent, we must pay an agency fee. We don't want to pay from our own money. We also know that if we add the agency fee to the sales price, an agent told us it would be difficult to sell as the home would be overpriced for the market."

I also said, "God, I know nothing is impossible for you. You can do anything and everything. Bring someone to buy this house." I prayed like this for a few days. I wanted to hear from God that He would bring someone to buy our house before we sign a contract with the real estate agency.

Since nothing is impossible with God, I firmly believed God would bring someone to buy our house. Even though the house price mighty be higher than it should be, I believed He will bring someone to buy our house. After praying four days, God asked me a question. He said, "How did I teach you?"

I went to say, "Huh?"

He said it again, "How did I teach you?"

I said, "Huh?"

"Did I teach you to lie?"

"No!"

"Did I teach you to deceive others?"

"No!"

"Did I teach you to steal from others?

"No, absolutely not!"

Then He asked, "If you know I did not teach you to lie, deceive, and steal from others, why in the world are you asking me to steal from others?"

"Huh? What? When did I ask you to steal from others?"

"You've asked me to bring someone to buy your house for more than its worth. If I bring someone to buy your house for more than its worth, aren't you asking me to steal from another person?"

"WHAT?"

"That person who would buy the house from you could be one of my children, and you ask me to steal from one of my own."

Then my thoughts quickly moved into another direction. Then I said to God, "What about a nonbelievers?"

"I am not going to ask you to bring a believer to buy my house, but what about a nonbeliever? You can certainly bring a nonbeliever to buy our house, can't you?"

Then He said, "How old were you when you first believed? How old were you when you became my child?"

I said, "Ah… I was in my early thirties."

Then God said, "Do you think it would have been right for me to steal from you and give it to one of my children when you were not my child?"

With a shock, I said, "No, absolutely not!" I gave God this answer because I don't think it is right for God to steal from me and give it to a believer just because I am a nonbeliever.

Then God said to me, "Whoever buys your house may not be my child right now, but one day, that person may become my child, just like you became my child."

Wow! I realized what God was saying. I didn't know what I was asking from God. When I asked God to bring someone to buy our house for more than what it's worth, I was basically asking God to steal from others. When this reality hit me, I said to God, "God, I didn't know that's what I was praying to you." I realized my prayers were completely wrong.

> Then God revealed this scripture to me: "You ask and do not receive, because you ask with wrong motives."
>
> (James 4:3, NIV)

He showed me that my motive was totally wrong. I was so focused on not losing any money that I didn't care if anyone else loses money, believer or nonbeliever. My prayer did not consider anyone else but me. I did not even imagine for a moment that the buyer could have been me. If I was a buyer, I would not wish to pay more for a house than what it's worth.

I prayed a selfish prayer. My prayers were totally out of God's character. God revealed to me that as long as I prayed selfish prayer, He could not answer. He can't and will not contradict Himself by answering anyone's selfish prayers.

God Cares for All People

Then God shined His light upon these scriptures to remind me how He cares for nonbelievers.

> But love your enemies, do good, and lend, hoping for nothing in return; and your reward will be great, and you will be sons of the Most High. *For He is kind to the unthankful and evil.* Therefore be merciful, just as your Father also is merciful.
> (Luke 6:35–36, NKJV)

> For He makes His sun rise on the evil and on the good and sends rain on the just and on the unjust.
> (Matthew 5:45, NKJV)

> To love him with all your heart, with all your understanding and with all your strength, *and to love your neighbor as yourself is more important than all burnt offerings and sacrifices.*
> (Mark 12:33, NIV)

When I was a nonbeliever, He cared for me also just like the scriptures above state, but I forget who I used to be. I, once, was a nonbeliever too. Though some may not serve God right now, like I did, God cares for them dearly too. Though some may not serve God right now, they can become a child of God in the future, the same way that we once were nonbelievers. Our Father wants us to imitate Him—imitate His love for all mankind.

> "Therefore be imitators of God as dear children. And walk in love, as Christ also has loved us and given Himself for us, an offering and a sacrifice to God for a sweet-smelling aroma."
> (Ephesians 5:1–2, NKJV)

Far too many times, we make a huge mistake by thinking we are the most special people on earth because we serve a special God. Yes, the fact is that we are special people, but He doesn't want us to be puffed up, full of ourselves, and arrogant toward anyone. Being a child of a special God doesn't give us the right to ask God to take advantage of nonbelievers, but that's exactly what I did! I asked God to take advantage of nonbelievers for me.

Children of God have favor of God, but the favor of God doesn't come this way—stealing from someone else. His favor doesn't come in an unjust way. He will not take things away from anyone, believers or nonbelievers, unjustly to benefit a believer. He never will do that for anyone!

I sincerely repented of my sins of wrong prayers. When my husband came home that evening, I shared with him what God showed me. I let him know what God wanted from us. We decided not to use a real estate agent but decided to pray and trust God.

The next day, we didn't make selfish prayers. We changed our prayer. I prayed, "Father, as you know, we do not want to spend any more money by using a real estate agent, so we need to sell the house on our own. Father, bring someone to buy this house. Who did you prepare this house for? I know you prepared this house for someone. Bring this person forward to us."

I prayed the same things for four days. On the fifth day in the evening, I received a phone call from one of my friends. I shared with her that we needed to sell our house because we were moving to Seattle, Washington. My friend then told me, she heard that one of her neighbor's friends was looking for a house to buy. She said that she would find out whether they had purchased a home and follow up with me.

The next day, she called and said they had not bought a house yet, and that they would love to stop by our house to view it. The next day, they came to our house and they bought it on the spot! We received our answer from God within a week from our prayers. Hallelujah!

How amazing He is! We simply changed our prayers as God directed. When God is pleased with His children, His answer come so quickly as the speed of light. We didn't do anything special. We just prayed how God wanted us to pray—an unselfish prayer—with the right godly motives.

We didn't use a professional agent to sell our house. We didn't get help from a so-called expert. We got help only from God. God sold our house in only a few days!

As we shared how quickly we sold our house, people were amazed at this and asked, "How did you sell your house? I've tried selling my house for a long time, but I didn't have any success. How did you do that?" The only thing we could say to them was, "We prayed and trusted God." Then some people said to us, "We prayed too!" I didn't know why their house couldn't sell. Perhaps, just perhaps, they didn't pray according His will? I don't know.

Now this is the buyer's testimony. They mentioned to us that they were looking for a house for quite some time without any success. They desired to buy a house in our community, but they couldn't afford it. The home prices were a bit higher than they could afford.

They even shared with us that they told their real estate agent to hold a house in another community, even though deep inside they really didn't like it. They mentioned that if they couldn't find a house they liked within two days, they were going to buy the house that was being held for them. But just before they made their final decision, they found our house for sale. They were so happy to find our house and bought it right on the spot. This reminds me of the following scripture:

> "And we know that in all things God works for the good of those who love him, who have been called according to his purpose."
> (Romans 8:28, NLT)

I feel, it is important to explain to you how they were able to afford buying our house. The reason they were able to buy our house was they only needed to assume our mortgage. They were able to assume our mortgage because we use a VA loan to buy our house, and the new buyer also qualified to use a VA loan. The VA loan allowed other qualified VA loan buyer to assume the loan.

The new buyer only had to assume a shorter loan, twenty-seven and a half years, because we lived in the home for nearly three years. And when we originally financed our loan, the interest rate was two points lower than when we were selling our house to them.

So, the buyer was getting a wonderful deal. The buyer got to assume a lower interest rate and only needed to finance for twenty-seven and a half years rather than thirty years. We did have one condition for the buyer to meet—they needed to pay all the seller closing cost.

With this condition, they fully agreed to it. God brought the perfect buyer for us. Everything was worked out for both of us as God had ordained, and we only wind up spending eighty dollars of our money for closing cost.

God Loves All People

God lead me to more of His scripture and shone His light on it.

"Now this is the confidence that we have in Him, that if we ask anything according to His will, He hears us."

(1 John 5:14, NKJV)

We sometimes tend to misunderstand about the word "His will". We read it as though it only applies to believers, but His will also applies to nonbelievers. Well, I was not aware of this. After God revealed my prayer was a very self-centered prayer, I changed and started praying according to "His will".

I learned, His will for nonbelievers is not to be taken advantage of by believers. When we pray, we need to pray according to His will for all people, believers and nonbelievers.

He is kind to all men, believers and nonbelievers. Not only that, he even asks us to love our enemies and love our neighbors as ourselves. God wants us to love all people as ourselves. God says if we love our neighbors as ourselves, we will not steal from ourselves, we won't take advantage of ourselves, and deceive ourselves. Therefore, God says if we love our neighbors as ourselves, that is a far better offering and sacrifice we could ever bring to God.

> "To love him with all your heart, with all your understanding and with all your strength, and to love your neighbor as yourself *is more important than all burnt offerings and sacrifices.*"
> (Mark 12:33, NIV)

In closing, I hope and pray that you don't pray like I did. When you pray, you need to consider others as yourself. Then, and only then, your prayers will be answered quickly.

I deeply thank God for His love toward all people. If He did not reveal my selfish prayer to me, it may not have turned out well for us. Our merciful Father taught me to change my selfish prayer. He guided me to pray according to "His will", His laws, so He could answer my prayer.

Our Father asked me to write this testimony to share with you, so you would know how to pray. Our Heavenly Father is anxious to answer all your prayers, but please check your prayers. Are your prayers selfish prayers? With the wrong motives? Do you just pray to get the best deal only for yourself? Do you pray like I did? When you pray, do you disregard everyone else?

Now you know God can't answer wrong motives, selfish prayers. It goes against His personal character. Though He is eager to answer your prayer, He cannot if your prayers violate His principles.

Please pray with love. Pray according to His will. Pray like how you would want others to treat you, then your prayers will never go out of His will. Your prayer will always be heard by your Heavenly Father. If your prayer of faith is working through love, you'll receive an answer from God always.

For in Christ Jesus neither circumcision nor uncircumcision avails anything, but faith working through love.

(Galatians 5:6, NKJV)

You ask and do not receive, because you ask with wrong motives.

(James 4:3, NIV)

Now this is the confidence that we have in Him, that if we ask anything according to His will, He hears us.

(1 John 5:14, NKJV)

As God is alive, His word is alive. And His "Word" will prove to you, He is alive.

9

When Did I Say, "I Will Prosper?"

One day, the Spirit of the Lord began to minister to me. "Why do you have a hard time obeying me?" When He asked me this question, I paused for a moment and listened again as He said, "You have trouble with obeying me. You obey me with much hesitation and delay."

When He said this to me, He was right about my unwillingness to obey. I knew, I had this problem before God even mentioned it to me. It didn't surprise me because I already knew I had an issue about my delay of obedience.

This whole discussion started like this. During this time, I needed to send some finances to one of our family members, and it caused me to noodle on things that consistently kept repeating in my life. I found myself asking this question, "Why in the world does my life have to be like this all the time? I could not remember, not even once, when I received anything from anyone? Somehow, I always had to be the one who gave to other people."

And as I thought about this, this seemed so unfair and made me quite upset and puzzled. The more I thought about this, I kept saying to myself "This seems so unfair. Why? Why do I have to give all the time? How come they can't give to me sometimes? How come I always give and never receive?"

I found myself going down memory lane and remembering how someone's face got lit up when I gave them money or a gift. They expressed such happiness when I gave something to them. I was perplexed as I never had experience that moment in my life.

I never knew what it felt like to receive. *What kind of feeling is that? I wondered. If my giving makes them so happy like that, how come I never felt that happiness? Who gave to my family anything or gave me anything?*

I know what God says, "It is more blessed to give than to receive" (Acts 20:35), but up to this point in my life, everyone was telling me to give, give, and give some more. Especially in my life, I started giving since I was eight years old. It was at eight that I lost my biological father, and since that point, we suffered just to have something to eat daily.

Being that I was the oldest child, I learned to share whatever I had with my younger siblings. Sharing became my awareness and desire ever since my father died. It was during this difficult time I learned how important food and money were to survival, and I learned to save. But all my saving was primarily for my family and not for myself. Whatever I saved, I gave it to my mother to help take care of my younger siblings.

This situation continued even after I got married. We, my husband and I, gave more than we ever received. We sent money off to help both our families. We sent money to help others not because we had so much. We just didn't spend money on things that we wanted, or for items that our children wanted.

We denied ourselves from the pleasures of buying and enjoying new things. We often bought things that were considered absolutely necessary and inexpensive. This was how we were able to send money to others.

We denied ourselves from most good things because we tried to save as much as we could for our future, but what we saved, oftentimes, needed to be sent off to someone else who needed help. What we saved for us someone else got to enjoy.

This pattern of life was repeated constantly, and it wasn't limited to family members but also with friends too. We constantly gave more than we received from friends and to some people we really did not know all that well. At this point in my life, I couldn't recall anything we received from anyone, either material things or emotional things.

After I became a Christian, nothing changed in this area of giving. Instead, it seemed to me I had to give even more to others. All these thoughts were bottled up within me, and resentment started to settle in my heart. The resentment was this: whenever I obeyed God, it seemed like others were receiving benefits from God rather than me and my family.

Things such as tithing, offerings, volunteering at church, and sending missionary funds, paying more for lunch than others would be willing to pay, and continuing to send help to our family members. All these things seemed to benefit others and God.

So, it led me down the path to have only one absolutely thought at this point in my life, "God asked me to obey Him for the benefits of others and the pleasure of God." It was this thought that caused me to delay obeying God.

After He said I have a troubled with obeying Him and with much hesitation, God asked me, "Do you think others received more blessing from me when you obey?" When He asked this, I was quite surprised. I understood that He knew of my hesitation of obedience, but I didn't know He knew the very reason why I delayed obeying, but God knew my exact reason.

Then God said, "When did I ever say to you, when you obey me that others would receive a blessing from me? When did I ever say to you when you obey me, I will be the one who receive benefits? Where did I say that to you?"

I knew He knew all my thoughts, but I was in utter shock! With this series of questions, He helped me take a deep look inside my heart. Then He said, "I want you to relook at some scriptures all over again." As usual, God led me to these scriptures.

> And now, Israel, what does the Lord your God require of you, but to fear the Lord your God, to walk in all His ways and to love Him, to serve the Lord your God with all your heart and with all your soul, and to keep the commandments of the Lord and His statutes which I command you today for your good?
>
> (Deuteronomy 10:12–13, NKJV)

"And now, what did I say?" God asked me. "Did I ask you to obey me for the good of others or for the good of you?"

I said, "For my own good."

Then God moved on to:

> "Oh, that they had such a heart in them that they would fear Me and always keep all My commandments, that it might be well (Prosper) with them and with their children forever!"
> (Deuteronomy 5:29, NKJV)

"Didn't I say when you obey me, everything will be 'well' with you and your sons forever?"

I said, "Yes, you did."

After this, I didn't know what to say. I had to be completely honest to God that I was wrong again. God went on:

> That you may fear the Lord your God, to keep all His statutes and His commandments which I command you, you and your son and your grandson, all the days of your life, and that your days may be prolonged. Therefore hear, O Israel, and be careful to observe it, that it may be well with you, and that you may "multiply greatly" as the Lord God of your fathers has promised you—"a land flowing with milk and honey."
> (Deuteronomy 6:2–3, NKJV)

"Whose days will be prolonged?" He asked?

"My days."

"Who may multiply greatly?"

"I."

I do not know what happened to me! Somehow, I thought when I obeyed God, other people received more blessings from God than me! I was completely off track in my thinking. What I forgot was that my obedience opened God's blessing for my life and not for others. God clearly says, "If I obey," I am the one who would eat the good of the land. And I did! But I forgot!

> "If you are willing and obedient, You shall eat the good of the land."
> (Isaiah 1:19, NKJV)

I didn't know what happened to me. I obeyed God but with much delay. I wasn't willing. I obeyed God because I had to do it, not because I loved to obey God, or I wanted to obey God, but because I obeyed God as an obligation; I obeyed God with a grumbling heart. I forgot what God said, "The willing and obedient" heart will receive all God's blessing. I obeyed God with much delay and not with a willing heart!

I was just like Israel! Israel experienced many wonderful miracles, but each time they face a challenge, they grumbled and complained against God. They grumbled because they forgot all the miracles God had performed for them. I, too, experienced many of His miracles, but I, too, also forgot about all the miracles of God and grumbled. I lost my willing heart to obey God.

I forgot, I am the one who receives blessings from God for my obedience. Somehow, I started to believe others were receiving blessings from God for my obedience. I was totally foolish thinking this way! This was a total deception for me. I asked God for forgiveness of my sins for not obeying quickly for the love of Christ and love for myself.

Because, we, Christian use phrases like, "Serve others, forgive others, lay down yourself for others, give your tithes, give your offerings, and send missionary funds to help others." After a while, we tend to think we are doing all these things only for others, but this is actually for our blessing! Our obedience opens God's blessings mainly for our lives and not for others.

You should never hesitate to obey God, like I did. In due season, you will receive the fruits of your obedience, not disobedience.

He requires your obedience for your good, your long life, your prosperity, and your well-being.

A faithful man or woman will be richly blessed not based on who is eager to get rich but a "faithful person". Be a faithful person. In the Bible, the people who received so much blessing from God were faithful and obedient to God. God wants your obedience for your blessing, not for someone else's blessing but for yours.

> "A faithful person will be richly blessed, but one eager to get rich will not go unpunished."
> (Proverbs 28:20, NIV)

Let's not forget the consequence of King Saul. He knew exactly the will of the Father. God told him what God wanted him to do, but Saul did what he wanted to do. Saul experienced God's miracles many times over. He knew God was the one who had made him the king of Israel, but his continual disobediences to God brought wrath on him and to his family. You know, God doesn't want the sacrifice of worship but of obedience.

> "Has the Lord as great delight in burnt offerings and sacrifices, As in obeying the voice of the Lord? Behold, to obey is better than sacrifice, And to heed than the fat of rams."
> (1 Samuel 15:22)

God says that He is delighted when we obey His voice rather than anything we offer. God doesn't want worthless sacrifices, worthless services of worship. God clearly lets us know what He requires of us. God requires our obedience coupled with a willing heart.

Again, your obedience is and will be for your blessings, it is for yours and your sons forever. Ever since I received this revelation from God, I continually repeat this to myself. "I will obey the Word of God for my blessing. I will obey the Word of God for my family's blessing."

So why not repeat this to yourself every time you run into difficulty of obeying God!

"I WILL OBEY THE WORD OF GOD FOR MY BLESSING. I WILL OBEY THE WORD GOD FOR MY FAMILY'S BLESSING."

Now, determine this in your heart to obey Him for your blessing.

> Walk in obedience to all that the Lord your God has commanded you, *so that you may live and prosper and prolong your days* in the land that you will possess.
> (Deuteronomy 5:33, NIV)

> The Lord commanded *us to obey* all these decrees and to fear the Lord our God, so that *we might always prosper and be kept alive*, as is the case today.
> (Deuteronomy 6:24, NIV)

Salvation of God is only possible when you "confess with your mouth the Lord Jesus and believe in your heart that God has raised Him from the dead, you will be saved." But the blessing of God is through your obedience! Do not hesitate to obey God! Your obedience is for your blessing, not for others.

> *As God is alive, His word is alive. And His "Word" will prove to you, He is alive.*

10

Free from Addiction: Some Interest

I was a heavy smoker and was very addicted to nicotine for many years. The first thing I did when I woke up in the morning was lit a cigarette. Then I went to the kitchen to grab a cup of coffee with sugar and cream in it. I was also addicted to strong caffeine. Like most smokers can relate to this, coffee with sugar and cream goes perfectly well with a cigarette.

Then, I sat in the living room and started to smoke and drink coffee. In one sitting, I usually had two cups of coffee and smoked a few cigarettes. Sometimes up to three cups of coffee with cigarettes. I could fast from a meal for few days, but I could never ever skip smoking cigarettes. Therefore, it didn't matter what was going on in my life. I made sure I never ran out of cigarettes.

After I became a Christian, a follower of Jesus Christ, baptized by His Holy Spirit and speaking in tongues, I continually smoked cigarettes. I never try to quit because I enjoyed smoking. As a matter of fact, whenever I had a visitor from church, I was not ashamed to light a cigarette in front of them. If that visitor happens to be a smoker, we smoked together. I was not embarrassed, nor did I try to hide it from people. I lit the cigarette unabashedly in front of anyone.

After seven years being a Christian, I was still smoking cigarettes. However, slowly, I started to have a little concern for fellow Christians, nonbelievers, and their perception of me. I began to feel a little bashful to light cigarettes in front of them. I started to be concerned about how they would think of me as a Christian.

So, I found myself more and more pretending like I was a nonsmoker. For instance, whenever I smoked, if someone walked toward me, I quickly put out the cigarette, or I quickly walked away from them to finish smoking. The habit of smoking a cigarette began to bother me as a seven-year-old Christian. I thought about quitting, but I never did try.

Lung Infection

Finally, I had a reason to quit. One day, when I had a cold, my lungs were infected with bronchitis. I went to the hospital and received medication for it. Then about a month later, again I caught another cold and bronchitis. By this time, I didn't like the fact that I contracted bronchitis twice within two months.

I had deep thoughts about quitting cigarettes. Then, once and for all, I decided to quit smoking. I prayed to God to help me quit, and I put on a nicotine patch to prevent nicotine cravings. But in couple of hours, I surrendered to the nicotine craving and started to smoke again.

About two weeks after my first attempt, I tried to quit again. I prayed to God to help me quit smoking, threw away all my cigarettes, and put on another nicotine patch. A few hours later, again, my body was crying for nicotine, especially when I had a cup of coffee. Well, I began to look for cigarette butts all over the place, in the astray, in the living room's trash can, and even in the kitchen's trash can.

I know this sounds yucky, but anyone who has been addicted to cigarettes would understand what I'm talking about. When I found a cigarette butt, I acted as though I've found a buried treasure. I lit it immediately and drew that toxic nicotine into my lungs. I drew it in as though I was starving for food for a long time. Once again, I tried but failed! I was disappointed for a moment, but I went back to smoking again as usual.

Another two months passed, I caught another cold again, and well, as you may have guessed it, I got the bronchitis too! This was the third time I caught bronchitis within four months! Now, I paid close attention to the sound of my body. My body was telling me that my lungs were not as strong as before.

This time, I had real concern. I began to have some fear about my health. I realized, I must quit immediately as possible. I knew, I had to be serious about quitting. Again, I threw out all my cigarettes, put on another nicotine patch, and prayed to God to help me with this.

This time, I decided to apply someone's prayer example that was shared with me. In the past, I heard from a pastor on how he gave up smoking. He asked God that when he smells any cigarette smoke that he should have a severe headache. As a side note, this pastor overlooked that when he requested this from God over thirty years ago, people were able to smoke cigarettes everywhere, in and out of buildings, even inside airplanes, without any restrictions to smokers.

Well, according to what the pastor said, God did answer his prayer, but he made a huge mistake in his request. It so happened that whenever he was in a public place, where people smoked, he started to have severe headache. He said, he forgot to ask God, that he should have a headache only when he smoked cigarettes. He recommended to all of us that we should pray wisely.

Well, I didn't want to have any headaches like he had as that would be awful. So, I prayed, "God, help me to dislike the smell of cigarettes without a headache." I prayed like this because I didn't want to be attracted by its smell to tempt me to smoke again. I wanted cigarette smell to be distasteful to me as possible, so I wouldn't ever have a relapse."

I also prayed, "Lord, strengthen me from nicotine cravings. Help me with this craving. Strengthen me to not have any nicotine cravings, strengthen me from caffeine craving. Help me to minimize coffee consumption." I prayed this because my first two attempts failed due to nicotine cravings. Especially when I had a cup of coffee, my body was severely crying for nicotine. I didn't want to repeat this again.

The first two days, I did get nicotine craving, but amazingly, it was very minor. I had one or two cups of coffee, but the nicotine craving was not strong enough for me to look for cigarette butts all over the place. And when I went out to do some shopping with many smokers passing by right next to me, I was not tempted to its smell! Instead, just as I prayed, the smell was so disgusting to me!

I said, "That's what I used to smoke? Wow, something that smells like that? How in the world did I smoke those awful things?" Well, what did I know? In less than ten days, I succeeded! I was very surprised. From that point till now, I never smoked again! It has been a little more than twenty years, and I have never been attracted to its smell. Its smell is still so awful to me.

Then one day, I was wondering what was different this time. "Well, that's strange? I did the exact same things as the last two times I tried to quit. I prayed and put on nicotine patches, but how come this time it was so easy to quit? What was the difference? What made it so easy for me?" Then God revealed there was a huge difference in my prayers and attitude.

With the first two attempts, I made very simple prayers. "God, help me to stop smoking." I never mentioned to God how and what I wanted Him to help me with quitting smoking. But on the third attempt, my prayer was completely different. I prayed more in detail how and what I wanted God to help me. For nicotine and caffeine craving, I prayed for Him to strengthen me. For relapsing, I prayed that its smell would be as awful as possible for me.

God revealed to me the difference also in my attitudes. With the first two attempts, I tried to quit more for my perception than for my health! I thought I was doing it for my health, but I wasn't. God showed me how I really thought about quitting. I thought, "If it wasn't for the perception of others, I could still enjoy cigarettes, but now, I needed to quit because perceptions of others."

God also showed how I really thought about my health. "It is not that bad. Nothing is seriously wrong with my health that I really need to quit. I just caught bronchitis." God revealed, because I tried to quit more for my perception than my health, I subconsciously developed the attitude of being rebellious and unwilling. Therefore, I couldn't be successful. Then He led me to:

> "He is a double-minded man, unstable in all his ways."
>
> (James 1:8, NJKV)

He told me, the first two times, I was completely double-minded. That was the reason why I couldn't succeed. God was correct about my double-minded attitudes. Then He led me to two more verses.

> "But let him ask in faith without any *doubting*, for the one who *doubts* is like the surf of the sea driven and tossed by wind. For let not that man expects that he will receive anything from the Lord."
>
> (James 1:6–7, NIV)

The Holy Spirit revealed this scripture to me in this way. Verse 6: "But let him ask in faith without *some interest*, for the one who have *some interest* is like the surf of the sea driven by wind." You see, the first two times, I had some interest in quitting for my perception. I didn't have the full interest to do it for my health.

Deep inside my heart, I really didn't want to quit. As I mentioned, I was pretty upset that I needed to quit for others, Christians and non-Christians.

Deep inside my heart, I still wanted to enjoy cigarettes; therefore, I was double-minded and only had some interest in quitting; as a result, I couldn't be successful.

But then when I tried to quit the third time, I didn't have any of this attitude. When I caught bronchitis the third time, I truly was worried about my health. I was dead serious about quitting for my health. When I decided to quit smoking, it wasn't for other people's perceptions. It was purely all for my health, nothing but for my health. When God revealed it to me, I was very surprised because He was absolutely right about the difference in my attitude.

How about you? Are you addicted to a substance to get high? Addicted to gambling? I know someone who goes to the casino immediately after church service. She is seriously addicted to gambling. Are you addicted to pornography, the internet, social media, shopping, or video games?

Whatever it is, how many times has God impressed you to deal with it? Do you want to be free from addictions? You know, God can help you. Perhaps you did try to quit but failed. Maybe you feel it is useless to try again. You feel you can't help it.

Have you thought about that perhaps you failed because in some way, you still wanted to enjoy the addiction? You failed because you did not really want to quit for yourself. Instead, you tried quitting for another person, such as for your spouse or a family member.

You felt guilt and sorry for their suffering because of your addiction, but deep inside you felt rebellious and you were unwilling. Or perhaps you did really want to let it go, but then you had concerns that you may lose the moment of fun, the moment of excitement, or the moment of comfort. So, did you behave ambivalent to be free from addiction?

Perhaps you may be thinking that your addiction is not so bad compared to another person's addiction. It is not as bad as others have made it sound. Or perhaps you feel you can control your addiction better than other people; that you won't lose control like other people. Or, are you plainly justifying your addiction because the government legalizes the substance you are abusing?

Maybe you rather remain as an addict and stay in a miserable state because you're afraid of the unknown of facing new challenges. You may be afraid of dealing with withdrawal symptoms, discomfort, and relapsing. Or you may worry that people who you used to hang out with will reject you. You hesitate at even attempting to quit because of unknown future challenges.

Whatever the reasons or excuses you have, don't hesitate to be free from addictions. Take it to God. Tell God whatever concerns, whatever fear, whatever doubts, or whatever keeps you from being free from addictions. Tell God everything. He will help you. God will help you to overcome your addiction. He will assist you to overcome. He will provide His strength! You can only do it through His strength.

But don't be doubled-minded like I was the first couple of times I tried to quit smoking. Don't just have some interest, like I did. If you are double-minded and only have some interest, then you're already setting yourself up for failure. You can't be free from addiction by being double-minded. You can't be successful. But if you fully commit to do it, then God will help you to overcome it completely. Once and for all, you will be set free from it for forever!

> For I, the Lord your God, will hold your right hand, Saying to you, "Fear not, I will help you."
> (Isaiah 41:13, NKJV)

> (God) will keep in perfect peace all who trust in (God), all whose thoughts are fixed on (God)!
> (Isaiah 26:3, NLT)

> For the eyes of the Lord range throughout the earth to strengthen those whose hearts are fully committed to him.
> (2 Chronicles 16:9, NIV)

Fully commit to be free from your addiction and God will keep you and help you with His peace and His strength. You will overcome it! You will be set free. If you fully commit to do it, then the power of God will strengthen you.

When I was double-minded about quitting smoking, God revealed to me that the power of God was not able to strengthen me. The Holy Spirit knew I still had a deep desire to smoke cigarettes. Since He knew, I really didn't want to quit, He couldn't empower me to quit. He waited until I was completely committed to do it. When I was fully ready and wasn't doubled-minded, the Spirit of God gave me all His strength to overcome all temptations.

As I mentioned earlier, I had very minor cravings for nicotine and caffeine because of His strength. I wasn't enticed by cigarette smoke because of His strength. The Holy Spirit provided all His power and strength to help me overcome any temptations. This is how I was able to quit within ten days and have never been tempted by it anymore.

> "I can do all things through Christ who strengthens me."
> (Philippians 4:13, NKJV)

It is vital to have a willing attitude. If you have an unwilling attitude and are doubled-minded, then the power of Holy Spirit will not and cannot strengthen you. If you just pray to see whether you'll be set free from the addiction, His strength and power will not work for you. You need to commit to do it. Then God will remove all the temptations out of you. And in case you are tempted, the power of God will strengthen you to overcome it.

If you try to overcome any addiction with your own willpower and strength, this is not enough for you to overcome. Some people might be able to overcome this way, but most people don't. Your willpower and strength can only sustain you for so long. It will most likely run out within a few hours or a couple of days, but through His strength and power, you'll overcome it! You'll be set free from your addiction! Just don't be double-minded and have only some interest!

> "Not by might nor by power, but by My Spirit,
> Says the Lord of hosts."
> (Zechariah 4:6b, NKJV)

Next, tell God exactly how you want Him to help you and what you want Him to help you. Let God know of your concerns, worries, fears, and doubts, or whatever it is. If you worry about relapse, let God know of it too. Tell Him as I did. Tell God how you want God to help you and what you want Him to help you. Take it to God. Lay it all to Him. He will help you and will carry it for you.

> "Then Jesus said, 'Come to me, all of you who are weary and carry heavy burdens, and I will give you rest'."
>
> (Matthew 11:28, NLT)

Again, I do not mind repeating myself to help you. Just don't be doubled-minded. Don't just have some interest. It is essential to have a willing attitude. If you are serious about it and fully committed to do it, God is more than happy to give you all His strength and power to overcome your addiction. You will be successful in Jesus's name.

> "Commit your actions to the Lord, and your plans will succeed."
>
> (Proverbs 16:3 NLT)

As God is alive, His word is alive. And His "Word" will prove to you, He is alive.

11

Pastor Black: Testing of Faith

This testimony happened when my husband lost his first job and found out he had hepatitis C. (Both incidents happened at the same time). At this time, we were very vulnerable from any of the enemy's attack. One battle is hard enough to deal with, but we were in two huge battles. My husband and I were under such pressure during this time in our lives.

The future was very uncertain to us, but even though the future was very uncertain, we didn't share our situation with anyone. So, we didn't receive any help from any family members nor from friends. Every time we went out shopping, we had to watch very carefully how we spent money. Although we didn't suffer from lack of finances, we didn't have what we used to have to buy things comfortably.

The things we used to buy so easily, now required us to give more thought before we picked it up. My husband and I just decided to trust God to provide for us. We knew there was no better person than God to put all our trust in. We also knew very well what we must do—pray!

It was a little past two months of unemployment when we received a prayer request from Pastor Raymond, who is one of our friends. He asked us to pray for one of the pastors that he knew. His name was Pastor Black, a pastor from Jamaica.

Pastor Raymond told us that Pastor Black was in the hospital for surgery. He needed some finances to pay for his surgery and other bills that had accumulated. We never met Pastor Black, but my husband and I decided to pray for him. We asked the Lord to meet all his needs.

One morning, when I was praying, the Lord gently reminded me of this scripture.

> What does it profit, my brethren, if someone says he has faith but does not have works? Can faith save him? If a brother or sister is naked and destitute of daily food, and one of you says to them, "Depart in peace, be warmed and filled," but you do not give them the things which are needed for the body, what does it profit?
>
> (James 2:14–16, NKJV)

When He revealed this to me, I knew instantly what God wanted us to do concerning Pastor Black other than praying. As a matter of fact, I knew what God wanted us to do for Pastor Black from the very beginning of my prayers, but I was not willing to listen to the Lord because I had a good excuse. My excuse was, we too are also in need of finances.

We did not suffer for meeting our monthly expenses, but we did not have any extra either. We were just meeting our monthly needs. This was the excuse; I reasoned as to why I ignored the voice of God. I just prayed to God to meet Pastor Black's needs through someone else but not through us, someone who had a lot more money than us.

When the Lord spoke James 2:14–16 to me, I could not pretend like I did not hear Him anymore. I couldn't pretend like I didn't know what God wanted from us. I needed to face the truth. I knew very well that God uses His people to meet the needs of others, but I didn't want to listen to God. I wanted God to understand our situation, being unemployed, but His words strongly convicted me to do something for Pastor Black.

> "If a brother or sister is naked and destitute of daily food, and one of you says to them, 'Depart in peace, be warmed and filled,' but you do not give them the things which are needed for the body, what does it profit?."
>
> (James 2:15–16)

Just as the scripture says, I prayed for Pastor Black's needs to be meet by someone else, but not through us. I wanted someone else to provide for his needs, so that's what I prayed. I thought I didn't have enough money for us, much less for anybody else.

I thought, I am not the one responsible for his needs. I wanted someone else to be responsible for his needs, someone who had a lot more money than me, but God revealed to me that I was the "someone else" to give what Pastor Black needed.

I shared it with my husband, and we decided to help Pastor Black. We prayed to see how much the Lord wants us to send. The next day, I prayed to God. "Father, as you know, my husband has not been working for two months. We do not have much to send but whatever you tell us to send, we will do it."

Though I asked God to reveal how much He wanted us to send, I felt a little uneasy. I felt uneasy because I worried that God might ask us to send more than we could; more than my faith could handle, but we still prayed for a few more days until the Lord revealed to me $300 with an understanding.

My understanding was that $300 was not so much in the United States, but in Jamaica, it is worth so much more. This amount would provide Pastor Black many benefits. And what God asked us to send wasn't too much for our faith to handle. The next day, I asked my husband how much the Lord had spoken to him about giving. The amount my husband told me was the same amount that Lord revealed to me—$300.

We were happy to obey God because we believed God would also meet all our needs too. We prayed over that offering and sent it to Pastor Black. After the money was sent, about three weeks, we received our answer from the Lord! My husband found a job in Oregon.

The amount God asked us to send to Pastor Black was so small compared to what we had received from God. Additionally, during these three months of unemployment, we never had to go to the bank to withdraw any money; not a single dollar was withdrawn to support our family. God met all our needs. "Praise the Lord."

Through this experience, I had noticed something very special—a repeating pattern of sowing and reaping. Whenever we needed answers from the Lord on finances, God always told us to sow in the area we need to reap. God had asked us to sow our finance to someone who is in need or into the church. As we sowed in this area, oftentimes, we received our answer within a couple of weeks.

I realized this was the "testing of our faith". Through the test, God wanted to see our faith. He tested us to see whether we truly believed Him for finances.

The first time it happened was when my husband had to change his career. God revealed to me that Pastor Raymond had needs and to sow finances into his life. We obeyed and then we received our answer!

I'll give you more details on this. When my husband retired from the Military, we prayed for a job. Close to two months had passed and God revealed to me, during my prayer time, that Pastor Raymond was in some kind of trouble or in difficulty.

During my devotional time, I usually prayed in sequences. First, I prayed for our church leaders, then on to friends and extended family, and my own family, and so on. As I was praying for Pastor Raymond, I felt such an excruciating headache that I couldn't pray for him anymore. So, I moved on to pray for his wife, Lisa.

When I prayed for her, all of a sudden, such deep sadness grabbed my heart and tears were running down on my cheeks. I quickly moved my prayers for someone else to alleviate myself from such strong pain and sad emotions. I didn't understand why this was happening to me, but I knew something was quite not right with them.

The next day, during my devotional time, the same thing happened again—excruciating head pain and deep sadness with tears. It was during the third day that I finally received some understanding of this situation. I felt such an excruciating headache because Pastor Raymond was dealing with so many difficult issues.

But I still didn't really understand why I felt such sadness, and tears were running down my cheeks, but I knew something was very wrong with them. After my prayer time, I shared it with my husband and asked him to contact Pastor Raymond to find out what's going on with them.

The next day, my husband shared with me that Pastor Raymond was facing some huge difficulties. He was dealing with three major problems. One, his father-in-law, Lisa's father, just passed away, but he didn't have money to send Lisa to Texas to attend her father's funeral. Two, because he just had surgery, he was unable to preach to local churches, thus not being able to receive an honorarium to support his family. And three, because he had no money coming in, he missed a few months of rent and received an eviction notification to move out soon. I leaned through my husband why I felt such an excruciating headache and great sadness.

Then we immediately knew why God revealed this to us. He wanted us to help them. The next day, we took all these issues in to our prayer. We prayed for a few days to find out how much God want us to send. Then the Lord told me to send $1000 to Pastor Raymond.

I asked my husband how much he heard from God. At first, he said $200. Then, I said, "Are you sure? I heard a thousand dollars." Then he said, "You are right, I heard a thousand dollars too, but don't you think it is too much?" Later, my husband revealed to me why he said only $200. He did not want to burden me with high amount since he was unemployed at the time.

So, $1000 was a bit too much for anyone who is not working. Even now, $1000 is much to many people. To be honest, it was a bit too much for both of us! At that time, our rent was only $650, included everything except electricity. The $1000 was one and half months of rent for us, but we still sent it out of obedience to God.

We obeyed God to send it out in the midst of no income because we believed God would provide all our needs. This was the testing of our faith.

> "Knowing that the testing of your faith produces patience."
>
> (James 1:3, NKJV)

The test was, although my husband didn't have a job and we had no steady income, if we truly believed God would answer our prayers for a new job, we could send what God requested us to send. God knew we had some emergency savings. So, God knew we could send the amount that He told us to send.

We sent this amount in the midst of unemployment! And passed the test. We sent it because we believed God would provide a wonderful job that He promised. And He did! Praise the Lord! He did more than enough! (Please read the first Job story).

God tests our faith to see whether or not we truly believe Him. People say that they believe God will take care of them, but whenever God provides an opportunity to prove their faith, they don't have any faith to prove it to God. They say they believed God will meet all their needs, but they don't show God they really believe Him. They don't sow into the area God shows them to sow to prove their faith.

Many of them fail the testing of their faith. Many are merely talkers of faith. Faith is not a word but an action. If you truly believed God will meet all your needs, then you should not have any problems to prove that faith to God.

> "For as the body without the spirit is dead, so faith without works is dead also."
>
> (James 2:26, NKJV)

Don't be alike some people, who pick and choose what scriptures they want to believe.

> Ask, and it will be given to you.
> (Matthew 7:7, NKJV)

> "Bring all the tithes into the storehouse, That there may be food in My house, And try Me now in this," Says the Lord of hosts, "If I will not open for you the windows of heaven And pour out for you such blessing That there will not be room enough to receive it."
> (Malachi 3:10, NKJV)

You see, you can't have selective faith and live victoriously. Matthew 7:7 doesn't require anything other than to pray, but Malachi 3:10 requires your finance to prove your faith. Many of us want to believe what does not require an effort or sacrifice. Many wanted to believe what does not cost them anything. They believe God selectively, but selective faith can't and will not be able to receive any of God's blessings.

We can't believe God's Word conveniently nor selectively. Faith does not, will not, and cannot work like that. We must believe all His Words. If we believe, we'll receive His blessings through obedience, then we must also know that we will receive disasters, curses, through our disobedience. Therefore, whether it costs us or not, we must obey God in and all to receive His blessings. We must follow all His principles to receive all the good things from God.

Do you remember the widow of Zarephath? How she first made the bread for the prophet Elijah? And you know, she only had a handful of flour and the last drop of oil. It was barely enough for her and her son to eat their last meal. There was no more meal to eat after that. That was the reason why she said they would eat and then die. But the Prophet Elijah told her:

> "For thus says the Lord God of Israel: 'The bin of flour shall not be used up, nor shall the jar of oil run dry, until the day the Lord sends rain on the earth'."
>
> (1 Kings 17:14, NKJV)

This was the "Testing of her faith". If she really believed in the Word of God, she would do as the prophet Elijah told her to do. She believed what the prophet told her. Instead of holding on to that little she had, she decided to trust God. She trusted God to sow into Elijah. God asked her to sow into Elijah's needs, so God could also meet her needs. God wanted to see her faith. And she showed she did believe God!

As long as she provided the prophet's needs, God also supplied all of her needs. Because of passing the "testing of her faith," during a severe drought, she saved her and her son's life by trusting and obeying God."

Let's think about it little deeper. Jesus says:

> But I tell you truly, many widows were in Israel in the days of Elijah, when the heaven was shut up three years and six months, and there was a great famine throughout all the land; but to none of them was Elijah sent except to Zarephath, in the region of Sidon, to a woman who was a widow.
>
> (Luke 4:25–26, NKJV)

There were many widows during this time in history, and perhaps, some of them may have had much more food than this widow. God could have sent Elijah to another widow who had much more food, but God chose this widow who only had the "last drop of oil and a handful of flour".

God knew; oh yes, God knew which widow had more than her. You see, God absolutely did not want her last bit of flour and the last of her oil! No, God could have chosen another widow to meet the needs of Elijah, but God chose her! It was the testing of her faith.

If, perhaps, she had refused to obey God, what do you think God would have done for Elijah? God would have sent Elijah to another person to take care of him and blessed them, and she would have missed her entire blessing. Her and her son would have died as she said. Therefore, it was nothing, but the "Testing of her faith".

Because she chose to obey God, she received her miracle. The same holds true for our situation. God could have asked someone else, who had more money than us, to send money to Pastor Raymond and Pastor Black, but God choose us to do it. It was nothing but the "Testing of our faith" to bless us. "Hallelujah."

When you are in a difficult situation, like that widow, or like my husband and I, it is not easy to obey God, but if God asked you to do something in the midst of your difficulty, you must understand this fact, it is the "Testing of your faith". It is not a testing of your faith if God asks you to give out of your abundance. (To give out of abundance to very stingy people, maybe testing of their faith). But if God asks you to give out of your own necessity, then it is the testing of faith.

Whenever you face the testing of your faith, you need to be very wise to understand, He knows who has way more than you. And remember, "Testing of your faith" is the evidence that your answer is closer than you think it is.

You see, God does not want your money. He wants your faith. If God needs money, He Knows who has way more money than you. He knows where the money is. But if he asks you to sow from that little you have, He just wants to see your real faith in action to bless you. Don't be a talker of faith but please be a walker of faith. You know, faith is the only element that pleases the Father to bless you and to do so openly.

> "But without faith it is impossible to please Him, for he who comes to God must believe that He is, and that He is a rewarder of those who diligently seek Him."
>
> (Hebrews 11:6, NKJV)

Don't hesitate in obeying the testing of your faith. If God speaks to you to sow, don't try to hold onto that little you have. Don't try to hold on to it. It will not last long. It is not enough to sustain your life. It will run out eventually, but if God chooses you instead of someone who has more money to sow, trust God to sow in the area that He shows you to sow. If you obey, it will not run out like that widow.

Remember, He will not ask you to sow more than your faith can handle. He knows how much your faith can handle and what you have. At first, when I prayed to God to see how much we should send to Pastor Black, I shared with you how I was afraid. I was afraid and worried that God might ask me to send more than my faith could handle, but God told us to send only $300.

God knew how much our faith could handle and how much we can send even in the midst of our financial difficulty. It was an important amount for us, but it was not enough to sustain our lives, nor it was too much to destroy our life. We decided to trust God, like that widow trusted God, to supplies all our needs. And He did!

Don't also make the mistake most people make in the area of finances. When they run into financial difficulty, they immediately withdraw from giving to God. That is one of the biggest mistake many people make. My husband and I gave a tithe to the Lord from our unemployment checks.

It wasn't enough for us. When shopping for groceries, we watched how many cans of food we picked up, and instead of buying two cans, we only bought one, but we made sure we gave our tithe onto God from our unemployment check. Action of our tithe in the midst of unemployment was to show God that we truly believed Him to bless our finances.

Well, I don't have any idea what you are going through right now. You might be struggling with finances like we did, but even in the midst of not having enough as you use to, if you can tithe to God, then give your tithe to God. Tithing is not optional, start showing God that you decided to trust Him for your finances. And if God's been asking you for something special to sow, obey His voice. This is the testing of your faith.

It is not the testing of my faith, not your friends' faith, or not your co-worker's faith. It is, "Testing of your faith." God knows who has more money than you. God could certainly ask that person to do it, but if God asks you to do it, it's because God wants to see your faith in action in order to bless you. Don't fail the "Testing of your faith".

These two-personal testimonies, I shared with you are both times my husband was unemployed. Both times, we were receiving unemployment checks. Both times, we asked God to help us to find employment. Both times, we were asking God for a financial breakthrough, and both times, God asked us to sow a financial seed. The first time was to Pastor Raymond, and the second time to Pastor Black. As we obeyed God, we received our answer, a new job from God within a couple of weeks. You can read both stories in this book.

I have many more testimonies in the financial area. And I will share them at a later time. One of the miracles is, how we paid off our entire mortgage even in the midst of unemployment! This is one of our greatest testimonies. Who could pay off their mortgage when one doesn't even have a job? But we did! Through the grace of God, we were able to pay off our entire mortgage. I love to share it in another story!

Don't be a selective believer. Don't use unemployment as an excuse not do what is right. Don't use excuses that others have more than you to not do what is right. God knows everything. He knows what you can do and what you cannot do. He knows what you have and what you don't have. If He asks you to do anything, He will ask you according to your faith and what you can handle to do.

What truth has been confronting you? Prove your faith to God. Without action, you can't see His Glory. Just remember, God can ask someone who has much more than you, but if He asks you to give from the little you have like that widow, then it is the "Testing of your faith." It is time to receive His blessing.

> Do you see that faith was working together with his works, and by works faith was made perfect… You see then that a man is justified by works, and not by faith only.
> (James 2:22, 24; NKJV)

> Jesus said, "Did I not say to you, if you believe, you will see the glory of God?"
> (John 11:40, NKJV)

As God is alive, His word is alive. And His "Word" will prove to you, He is alive.

12

First Job: Pray Specifically

When we moved to Washington State and lived there for about seven months, my husband decided to retire from the military. Normally, the military requires twenty or more years of service to retire, but during this time, the government was allowing a member to retire a little early having sixteen years or more of service. So, he decided to retire from the military after nineteen years of service.

But now, retiring from the military meant he needed to find a new job as soon as possible. Finding a new job was a very difficult thing to do for my husband because he had not been looking for a job for the entire time in the military.

Besides, we did not know anyone in Washington State who could help him find a job, nor we did have any family members who live close by us to help. Most of our family lived on the East Coast. The only one we had for sure was God. We had to fully depend on God to help us.

We began to pray to God about our situation. We prayed together and also separately for a new job. One day, as I was praying for my husband's job, the Lord asked me a question. "What kind of job do you want for your husband?" I was quite surprised and did not know what to say to Him. Again, He asked, "What kind of job does he want?"

Huh? What does He mean?

He went on to say, "How do you know if that the job your husband is going to receive comes from me?"

"I have no way of knowing whether it came from you."

He said, "You are right. If you ask for just a job, you don't know if it came from me. Since even nonbelievers also get jobs, there is no way for you to know if that job is from me. Both of you will think he naturally found a job just like nonbelievers do."

God continued, "And if you and your husband don't know for sure it is from me, both of you will doubt about the job when he runs into difficulties. Especially, your husband will doubt if he doesn't know for sure it came from me. If he knows for sure it is from me, he will not doubt and will endure any challenges and difficulties."

Then I said to God, "You are right! He could potentially think like that, since he has no way of knowing it came from you." Wow! God is so thoughtful and so detailed.

When I got this revelation from God, I finished my prayer. That evening, I asked my husband what kind of job he wanted from God. He told me he really doesn't know, but he desired to work as a marketing person. He has never worked in that area before.

The next day when I prayed, I told God what my husband wants from Him. I said, "Father, he wants to work in the marketing area, but there are so many different marketing fields. There is newspaper marketing, magazine marketing, TV marketing. There are so many marketing jobs that I don't know what to pray to you."

Then God told me, "Pray more specifically to know that the job is from me." Well, I thought, *Pray specifically?* I did not know how to pray specifically. Again, I told God, "I don't know what job to ask of you because there are so many different marketing jobs. I have no way of knowing what marketing job to ask of you."

Then again, God told me. "Pray more specifically."

Again, I thought, *Pray specifically? Specifically on what? I don't know anything about marketing? How? And of what?*

Then all of a sudden, God told me, "Pray for a specific amount of income to earn." I paused for a while with a question, "Specific amount?" I was wondering about it and asked this question to myself,

"How much should I ask for? And what is the right amount?" I didn't have any idea how much to ask God. *"How much is the right amount to ask?"* All of a sudden, a certain number was rising from the inside of my heart. And I was in a huge shock!

This number was something I never imagined! There is no way this number was coming out of me. As a matter of fact, we were planning to thank God for any job. After all, my husband may not even have a job for a while! Therefore, we were going to accept any job that could help him earn the same or a little more income to maintain our current life style, but this number rising from inside me was a *hundred percent increase* from what my husband was currently making from the military!

I never thought or imagined praying for a hundred percent increase, but God initiated me to pray for a hundred percent increase. Wow, God is full of surprises!

With a shocked look on my face, I asked, "Are you sure of this?"

He said, "If your husband gets a job that pays that amount, both of you will know for sure that the job is from me. Both of you will know for sure that he did not fumble into the job just like non-believers. You'll know for sure it came from me."

I'll tell you, God is so amazing. He is awesome. Since God knew I didn't know how to pray specifically, He gave me specific instructions on the amount to pray for this job. So, I would know that the answer was from God.

Now, when I heard this amount from God, I knew one thing for sure, I could believe God for this amount. After all, He is the one who told me to pray for that amount, therefore, I knew for sure that God would do what he said He would do.

When my husband came home that evening, I shared with him what God had told me. As you can imagine, He was in a state of shock just like I was. My husband's jaw dropped to the floor. Okay, it is little bit of an exaggeration.

We decided to believe God and prayed for it. My husband and I made an agreement to pray for that amount and for a marketing job. We knew it was impossible for us to find a job that paid that amount, but we knew for sure that with God, everything is possible.

"For with God nothing will be impossible."
(Luke 1:37, NKJV)

Then we went through the Bible and wrote down some of God's finance promise scriptures in our notes. These are the scriptures that we meditated on day and night and made a faith confession each and every time we prayed.

> And my God shall supply all your needs according to His riches in glory in Christ Jesus.
> (Philippians 4:19, NKJV)

> Be anxious for nothing, but in everything by prayer and supplication with thanksgiving let your requests be made know to God.
> (Philippians 4:6, NKJV)

> In the same way God, desiring even more to show to the heirs of the promise the unchangeableness of His purpose, interposed with an oath. In order that by two unchangeable things, which it is impossible for God to lie, we may have strong encouragement, we who have fled for refuge in laying hold of the hope set before us.
> (Hebrews 6:17–18, NKJV)

> For I, the Lord, do not change; therefore you, O sons of Jacob, are not consumed.
> (Malachi 3:6, NKJV)

> "Bring whole tithe into the storehouse, so that there may be food in My house, and test Me now in this", saying the Lord of hosts, "if I will not open for you the windows of heaven, and pour out for you a blessing until it overflows."
> (Malachi 3:10, NASB)

> For as many as may be the promises of God, in Him they are yes; wherefore also by Him is our Amen to the glory of God through us."
>
> (2 Corinthians 1:20, NKJV)

Whenever I prayed, I read these verses to remind Him about His promises on our tithe and what He promised to us in our finances. I told God, we are expecting these promises to manifest in our life. We thanked Him for His promises and for His faithfulness to His Word.

Now, to those who have not been giving tithe to God, I recommend that you sincerely repent of it and begin to tithe. If not, the devil will condemn you for not tithing to God. The devil will try to persuade you to give up on your prayers for finances.

Devil will say to you, "It will not work for you because you did not tithe." But if you sincerely repent of it and begin to tithe, God will forgive you and show you His mercy on your finance situation. Don't give any opportunity to the devil to condemn you and consume you.

Visitation from the Enemy

We prayed every day jointly and independently. We believed God for a new job and new financial increase. But the enemy was not going to leave us alone. There were many nights the enemy tried to seize my attention to put fear in my heart and mind. He tried during many visits to influence me to change my faith, confession, and prayers.

Between the hours of 2:00 to 3:00 a.m., whenever I tossed around in my bed, all of a sudden, these types of thoughts came to me: "Oh my goodness, maybe I might be asking for too much from God. Maybe, I should just ask God for a job paying what my husband has been earning. It is much easier to find a less paying job. Higher paying jobs are far less available. It might take him too long to find a high paying job."

"We might not have much finance, but at least we can maintain our lifestyle just the same. Maybe I might need to change my prayer, so he can have a job, any job, as soon as possible." The enemy put all these crazy thoughts through my mind to change my confession and faith.

Meditation

I knew where these thoughts were coming from—the devil. Every thought I had contradicted as to what God told me to pray. Well, whenever I had these thoughts, I physically got up from bed and grabbed my notes and started to read the scriptures to meditate on them. As I read the scriptures, I reminded myself of what God said about the job and our finances.

After I read to meditate, I told God, "God! I know that you know what you said about your promises. I just read these scriptures to *remind myself* what you promise to us." Then I closed the notebook and thanked God and went back to sleep. And I slept like a baby for the rest of the evening.

Two months had passed, and we were in our third month of praying, but there was not even a single call for an interview, but we maintained our faith. It was not easy for us to deal with it. Think about it. Not a single call for nearly ninety days! A spiritual battle for ninety days. Night and day, twenty-four hours a day, we waited on a call from any company, but no calls!

And besides, the enemy was working overtime and came often to try to put fear and doubts in me. I felt a little uneasy, oh yes, uneasy for sure, but I maintained my faith by meditating on His words. Though many temptations came to change my faith and confessions and prayers, I still firmly believed God would do what He says he would do. I believed, "Ask and it will be given to you" (Matthew 7:7).

God Commanded Us

> This Book of the Law shall not depart from your mouth, but you shall meditate in it day and night, that you may observe to do according to all that is written in it. For then you will make your way prosperous, and then you will have good success.
> (Joshua 1:8, NKJV)

> Blessed is the man Who walks not in the counsel of the ungodly, Nor stands in the path of sinners, Nor sits in the seat of the scornful; But his delight is in the law of the LORD, And in His law he meditates day and night. He shall be like a tree Planted by the rivers of water, That brings forth its fruit in its season, Whose leaf also shall not wither; And whatever he does shall prosper.
> (Psalm 1:1–3, NKJV)

> For the weapons of our warfare are not carnal but mighty in God for pulling down strongholds, casting down arguments and every high thing that exalts itself against the knowledge of God, bringing every thought into captivity to the obedience of Christ.
> (2 Corinthians 10:4–5, NKJV)

As these scriptures direct, I meditated on His words from my notes before I prayed. I meditated on His words before I went to bed. I meditated on His words whenever the enemy put negative thoughts in my mind. By meditating on His words, I brought all the negative thoughts of the enemy into captivity and replaced the thoughts of evil to thoughts of faith and hope.

I constantly reminded myself of His promises. Through meditation of the words based on my notes, I let the peace of God to rule and reign in my heart. Through meditation, I remained in faith.

Word of Encouragement

I don't know what you are going through right now or what battle you are facing. Don't change your faith confession. Don't waver in your belief in God. The enemy will come to you as often as he can to destroy your faith. He will put fear and doubts into you to change your faith and confession. I recommend for you to do what I did. Write down His promises pertaining to your situation.

Read it and meditate on it daily. Through meditation, remind yourself of His promises. His words will strengthen your faith and give you real hope. If you meditate on His word, you'll not waver on your faith. Reject all negative thoughts through meditation. Replace all the negatives thoughts with His words and promises. And it will be done for you as you believe.

Manifestation

At the end of the third month, finally, we received a phone call from one company. Its headquarters was in Europe, and it just started to expand in the United States. They were interested in interviewing my husband. My husband went in and interviewed with several other candidates. Then he received a call a week later to interview for the second time and they offered him the job! We were so thankful to God and gave all the praises to Him. God did what He said He will do. He is so faithful!

Now, let's take moment to think about it. How in the world could this be possible? My husband was competing with other candidates for the position. Other applicants certainly had more marketing experience than my husband. How in the world could those people, who interviewed my husband, think that he would do a better job than those who had much more experience?

They knew my husband had not worked in the civilian job market for nearly twenty years. They knew my husband was a professional soldier. My husband disclosed all this information to them.

We knew for sure this was nothing but a miracle of God. We knew God's hands were all over the interview process. What was impossible for us, God made it possible for us. And I know one thing for sure, what God did for us, He can also do it for you too.

Negotiation of Salary

Now getting a job is one thing but it was another thing to get the salary that God told us we would get. My husband went in for the negotiation of his salary. They offered him two thirds of what we prayed for and an eight percent bonus from his total salary. Though the base salary was lower than what we prayed, but including the bonus, the total annual income was way more then what God told us to pray.

For some reason, their bonus structure doubled each month for six months, and on the seventh month, it started all over again for another six months.

For example, if the first month bonus was $500, then the second month bonus would be $1000, and the next month would be $2000 the next month $4000, and so on until the sixth month, and then on the seventh month, the bonus started at $500 again.

If this was true, our total income would be way more than what God told us to pray. We were in shock! It was much more than what we prayed! As we calculated some months, the bonus was more than the actual month's pay! With this offer, my husband accepted the job.

My husband began to work, but we were still confused with their bonus structure. Because as far as we knew, no company gives bonuses like this company. When we sat down to calculate it, and on the fifth month, the bonus was two times the amount of our monthly pay, and on the sixth month of bonus, it was a little over four times our monthly pay. This didn't make any sense to us. We thought either my husband didn't hear it right or they made a mistake of explaining the bonus structure.

So, my husband asked them to explain it to him three more times, but each time, they explained it the same way as before! We were still confused. So, I recommended to my husband to ask them for one final explanation. This time, the vice president and his office manager with a bit of frustration, wrote it down in my husband's notebook of how much bonus he would be receiving in the first month, second month, third month, and so on until the sixth month.

Well, we still didn't understand why they gave away so much bonus money, but if this company pays bonus like this, we were not going to complain. With this understanding, my husband kept himself busy with his work. He was learning lots of stuff. About four months of working, the chief finance officer of the European HQ discovered that they had made a huge mistake on bonus structure.

Bonuses were not supposed to pay out the way they were explained. They were not supposed to double up each month for six months. You see, some of their employee's base pay was a lot higher than my husband, so at the end of their sixth month, some were receiving massive amount of bonus.

They made a huge mistake and the company was facing an enormous panic. They were even concerned about potential lawsuits. They needed to renegotiate all seventeen US employees' salaries and bonuses. Well, we were in shock too. We were facing an unknown situation. We had an uneasy feeling. We didn't know what would happen, but we put all our faith and trust in God.

His coworkers also had many concerns as we had. The company's CEO, president, and vice president was working hard to renegotiate with their employees. One by one, they settled their salary and bonus issues, but no one was sharing anything to anyone.

Finally, my husband went in for his renegotiation. They apologized to my husband for the problem they caused, and then they went into renegotiation, but what they offered to my husband was much less than what they promised to pay him. My husband explained to them how much he was supposed to earn if they paid him as they contracted to pay him, salary and bonus.

Well, with the evidence what they wrote down to my husband note and salary contract, they couldn't argue with that point. They did try to pay him far less than what we prayed, but after several meetings, they decided to meet in middle. Now, you may have guessed it already; this middle point was the amount that God dropped in my heart to pray for. Hallelujah!

He is a faithful God. He never breaks His promises to His children. The Bible says every word that proceeds out of God's mouth never goes back to Him empty. You can rest assure that God will do what He says He will do. You just need to believe God for who He is and give thanks for His promises.

> "So shall My word be that goes forth from My mouth; It shall not return to Me void, But it shall accomplish what I please, And it shall prosper in the thing for which I sent it"
> (Isaiah 55:11, NKJV)

Why Should You Pray? He Knows Everything

You may think, since God knows everything, why you should even pray? You see, although God knows everything, He didn't say He will just give to you without you asking. God says you need to make a request unto Him.

> Thus says the Lord God: "On the day that I cleanse you from all your iniquities, I will also enable you to dwell in the cities, and the ruins shall be rebuilt. The desolate land shall be tilled instead of lying desolate in the sight of all who pass by. So they will say, 'This land that was desolate has become like the garden of Eden; and the wasted, desolate, and ruined cities are now fortified and inhabited.' Then the nations which are left all around you shall know that I, the Lord, have rebuilt the ruined places and planted what was desolate. I, the Lord, have spoken it, and I will do it." Thus says the Lord God: "I will also let the *house of Israel request of Me to do this for them*: I will increase their men like a flock."
> (Ezekiel 36:33–37, NKJV)

You see, God revealed His will to the people of Israel and made wonderful promises, but God required for the Israelites to ask God to do these things for them. Same as, although God knows all your needs, wants, and has made wonderful promises, God wants you to seek Him and make petition unto Him. God wants to see whether you truly believe that He is and that His promises are true. And if you truly believe that He is and His promises, you won't have any hesitation to ask Him.

> Be anxious for nothing, but in everything by prayer and supplication, with thanksgiving, *let your requests be made known to God.*
> (Philippians 4:6, NKJV)

> Until now you have asked nothing in My name. *Ask, and you will receive*, that your joy may be full.
> (John 16:24, NKJV)

> That night the Lord appeared to Solomon in a dream, and God said, *"What do you want? Ask, and I will give it to you!"*
> (1 Kings 3:5, NLT)

Although God knows everything, He still asked Solomon, *"What do you want? Ask, and I will give it to you!* Although Jesus knew everything, He asked blind Bartimaeus, *"What do you want me to do for you?"* (Mark 10:51, NIV). You see, God won't give to you without you asking. You must let your request be made known to God. You must ask God to show your faith, that you truly believe He is and His promises.

> "And without faith it is impossible to please God, because anyone who comes to him must believe that he exists and that he rewards those who earnestly seek him."
> (Hebrews 11:6, NIV)

Besides, if you do receive what you want without praying to God, how do you know it came from God? How do you know that? The devil will deceive you by saying, "You didn't receive it from God because you didn't ask it from God. You got it just as nonbelievers get it. God didn't give it to you because you never asked God to give it to you. You were just lucky to receive it." You see, this is another reason why God wants you to ask Him to make sure you know it came from God.

> "You lust and do not have. You murder and covet and cannot obtain. You fight and war. *Yet you do not have because you do not ask*"
> (James 4:2, NKJV)

Let me share with you one of my experiences. When one of our sons was a freshman in college, one day, he was in a such a rush to go somewhere. So, I asked him where he was heading out in such a hurry. He told me he was heading out to the school library to borrow a laptop to do his homework. I asked him why he didn't ask us to buy him a laptop. His answer was, he didn't think he needed it and he could still get by borrowing it from the school.

So, I asked, "Are you sure you don't need it? Do you really want to go through the inconvenience of borrowing every time you need it?" Then he finally told me, it will help him tremendously if he had one. So immediately, my husband and I purchased one for him.

You see, if he just simply asked us for it, he could have eliminated all the troubles of rushing to the library, borrowing it, and returning it at the proper time. He didn't have it because he didn't ask us for it. You don't have it because you didn't ask. So, ask God! He will give it to you.

Pray Specifically

Let's look at a Bible character who prayed specifically to God to receive what he needed. Abraham sent his chief servant to go to his country and to his relatives to find a wife for his son Isaac. When his servant arrived at the place called Nahor, he began to pray to God.

> I am standing beside this spring, and the daughters of the townspeople are coming out to draw water. "May it be that when I say to a young woman, 'Please let down your jar that I may have a drink,' and she says, 'Drink, and I'll water your camels too'—let her be the one you have chosen for your servant Isaac. By this I will know that you have shown kindness to my master."
> (Genesis 24:13–14, NIV)

He prayed specifically for what he wanted. So, he would know for sure Isaac wife is from the Lord. In this way, there is no ambiguity about Isaac's wife. But if he had said bring a woman to me, a woman may have come to him, but he would not know for sure that she was for Isaac and from God. Scripture say that the ladies of that town started to come to a well to draw water. This means there were many ladies.

So, who was supposed to be Isaac's wife—a woman at the well who made this servant feel good, or a woman who looked prettier than others? Or a taller one? Or a shorter one? There was no way of knowing who was for Isaac. This was the reason he prayed specifically to make sure Isaac wife was from the Lord.

Now, if you are already married before you knew this, you should not think that your spouse may not be the one from Lord. Once you are married, God still ordains your marriage in Christ. God sanctifies your marriage and your entire family by your faith.

> And a woman who has a husband who does not, believe, if he is willing to live with her, let her not divorce him. For the unbelieving husband is sanctified by the wife, and the unbelieving wife is sanctified by the husband; otherwise your children would be unclean, but now they are holy.
> (1 Corinthians 7:13–14, NIV)

Who Prayed Specific?

A synagogue leader:

> "While he was saying this, a synagogue leader came and knelt before him and said, 'My daughter has just died. But come and put your hand on her, and she will live'."
> (Matthew 9:18, NIV)

Blind Bartimaeus:

> "What do you want me to do for you?" Jesus asked him. The blind man said, "Rabbi, I want to see."
> (Mark 10:51, NIV)

Both men made a specific request to Jesus. The synagogue leader didn't ask Jesus just to come to his house and pray for his daughter. "But put your hand on her." Bartimaeus didn't say, "Just bless me, have mercy on me." Nor, he didn't say to Jesus, "How come you're asking me what do I want you to do for me? Can't you tell, I can't see? You should know what I need. So, shouldn't you just give to me without asking? You should know this. You are the Messiah." No, Bartimaeus told Jesus exactly what he wanted.

King Solomon:

> That night the Lord appeared to Solomon in a dream, and God said, "What do you want? Ask, and I will give it to you!..." Give me an understanding heart so that I can govern your people well and know the difference between right and wrong. For who by himself is able to govern this great people of yours? The Lord was pleased that Solomon had asked for wisdom.
> (1 Kings 3:5, 9–10, NLT)

Solomon didn't say, "Lord, you know all, you know what I need just give it to me." No, he told God exactly what he wanted, what he needed was the "wisdom" to govern His people. So, don't say, "God knows everything. He knows what I need," or don't say, "He will give to me, if He see I need it." No, you must ask God exactly what you need and what you want.

Let it be more specific. If not, you won't know where it came from. You may think you receive by coincidence. Throughout the Bible, God never spoke to His people in ambiguity. He always spoke with precise instructions and precise details. You must ask specifically to show your faith as the examples above.

Make Specific Prayer with Common Senses

Now we need to be also careful about specific prayer. When we overly specify about anything, we can tie God's hands. Common sense must be present when you ask God with specific prayers. For example, we did not ask God for a CEO position at Microsoft or the Boeing Company. Even if we had asked God, God wouldn't give it to my husband because God knew my husband was not ready to handle that type of position.

If you make specific prayers more than what you can handle or are ready for, God cannot answer that prayer. Because this is not faith but foolish faith. God does miracles on what you can handle or are ready for. Make specific prayers with common senses but not on greed, or on foolishness.

Don't Overly Specify

> Which of you fathers, if your son asks for bread, will give him a stone? Or if he asks for a fish, he won't give him a snake instead of a fish, will he? Or if he asks for an egg, he won't give him a scorpion, will he? If you then, being evil, know how to give good gifts to your children, how much more will your heavenly Father give the Holy Spirit to those who ask him?
> (Luke 11:11–13, NKJV)

If you need bread, pray for bread. Don't pray for rice, or generalize as you just need some food. Be specific, but don't overanalyze what kind of bread. Don't say it must be round, only six inches wide, a certain weight, and it must have a certain flavor. If you need fish, pray for fish; don't pray for meat. You may say what kind of fish, but don't overanalyze and saying it must be only from a certain ocean, size, weight, etc. Pray specifically but with common sense!

One more example of how to ask for a spouse. Don't ask that your spouse must be of certain height, weight, looks, employment, education, and salary. I met some people who asked this way. All these can change over time. If you overly complicate your prayers and say, "This is the only way," God can't answer your prayers. It is not because He can't, but He won't because you are not open to His perfect will of suggestion. Pray specifically but don't be overly specific. Make specific prayer with common sense.

Don't Know How to Pray Specifically?

Now you may say you don't know how to pray specifically about your situation. That is fine. Just start somewhere, like I did. I only told God what I knew. After I found out my husband wanted to work in the marketing field, that's what I told God. I knew nothing about marketing and what kind of marketing job was right for my husband. I knew nothing about it.

I just let God know only what I knew, and God totally understood that was the only information I had. When God suggested how much we should pray for, that's what we prayed. We prayed for a specific amount to earn, but we didn't pray for specific marketing field, but just marketing field.

God understands you have limited information on whatever you are asking, like I had limited information on marketing. But start at some point. If you a need job, don't just ask for a job. At least, let Him know what field, or area you want to work in, or how much you need or want to earn with common sense.

> "Ask, and it will be given to you; seek, and you will find; knock, and it will be opened to you."
> (Matthew 7:7, NKJV)

But remember this. A very and very important aspect of specific prayer is to open your heart to any of His suggestions. Listen carefully to your heart but not your mind. Please listen very carefully to your heart—your inner heart—where God reveals His thoughts. If you can listen to His suggestions carefully, you'll know His perfect will for your life. Then you know for sure how to pray more specifically according to His will for your life.

Now, God Is Asking You:

> "What do you want me to do for you?"
> "What do you want? Ask, and I will give it to you!"

As you seek His face, may the father of our Lord bless you and guide you into His perfect will. Amen.

> *As God is alive, His word is alive. And His "Word" will prove to you, He is alive.*

13
Hepatitis C

After my husband had been retired from military for about one and a half years, he found out that he had hepatitis C. We were in shock. We were devastated with this bad news. We didn't know what to think. We were already in one battle, but we were facing another battle in our lives at the same time. The first battle we were facing was my husband needed to look for a new job and at the same time he had to fight this horrible cancer.

We knew, we needed to take it to God. The next day, we began to pray. I let God know what we had discovered. I told God, "Father, as you know, we just found out my husband has hepatitis C. I want you to take care of this for us. As you know, Father, I am not afraid of my husband dying. If he dies, I know he will go to heaven, but my children and I need him here with us more than in heaven. My husband has to do lot more things on planet earth. So, Father, I asked you to take away this sickness from him."

Then suddenly, I heard it in my heart, "Bitter waters of Marah." *Bitter waters of Marah? What does bitter waters of Marah have to do with my husband's healing?* I didn't understand it. The only thing I remembered about the story of bitter waters of Marah was Moses and the people of Israel did not have water to drink for three days. When they came to Marah and found water, they couldn't drink it because it was bitter (poisoned).

Then Moses prayed to God, and God showed him a tree and commanded that he throw it into the water. Moses obeyed, and the water got sweet allowing the people to drink it. This was all I knew of the bitter waters of Marah. I didn't understand what the bitter waters of Marah had to do with my husband's healing, so I moved on and prayed for other people.

The next day, I prayed for my husband's healing, and once again I heard, "Bitter waters of Marah," but I still didn't get it and thought, *What does bitter water of Marah have to do with my husband's healing?* And just like the previous day, I moved on to pray for others.

On the third day, once again, I heard it from my heart, "Bitter waters of Marah." I knew right there and then God was trying to tell me something through this story.

I stopped praying and reached for my Bible. I did not remember the exact chapter, but I knew which book it was in; it was in the book of Exodus. I began to flip the pages and when I found it, I began to read to discover what God was trying to say to me.

> So Moses brought Israel from the Red Sea; then they went out into the Wilderness of Shur. And they went three days in the wilderness and found no water. Now when they came to Marah, they could not drink the waters of Marah, for they were bitter. Therefore, the name of it was called Marah. And the people complained against Moses, saying, "What shall we drink?" So he cried out to the Lord, and the Lord showed him a tree. When he cast it into the waters, the waters were made sweet. There He made a statute and an ordinance for them, and there He tested them, and said, "If you diligently heed the voice of the Lord your God and do what is right in His sight, give ear to His commandments and keep all His statutes, I will put none of the diseases on you which I have brought on the Egyptians. *For I am the Lord who heals you.*"
> (Exodus 15:22–26, NKJV)

When I ran across, "For I am the Lord who heals you," I was stunned for a moment! The whole time, God was trying to tell me He is "The healer," and He will heal my husband's disease. I learned this was the reason why God kept saying to me, "Bitter waters of Marah." At that moment, my heart was touched by His great love.

His love was like an indescribable hot boiling liquid. I felt like I could melt in His great love. Tears were running down my cheeks like hot water. It seemed like I had boiling pots of water in my heart because of His love. Other than what I written to you, how else can I describe His love to you? Words cannot express or describe the love I felt that day from our Heavenly Father.

As I was crying, I thanked God for His promising words and I asked, "Father, I thank you so much for your word. For the confirmation of this word, would you please give to my husband the exact scripture? My husband needs to hear it from you because he is the one physically ill and must go through the chemo treatment. He needs to know for sure that you spoke his healing. So, he will not falter whenever he feels it is too difficult to handle or too hard to deal with treatments. Give him the *same scripture* because it is not I, but my husband who needs to be strengthened in your promise."

I asked God for this because the cancer treatment was so exhausting. I knew my husband needed to hear it from God for assurance. After all, he would be the one who must go through such a challenging treatment. Therefore, I needed to make sure he heard from God for his healing.

My biggest concern was, if my husband didn't hear from God, the devil could deceive my husband and prevent him from receiving his healing. I prayed for this so that the devil would not steal the healing promise from us.

At this time, my husband was battling with three issues—this deadly disease, looking for a new job, and the enormous pain in his heart from people who hurt him from his former company. For all these reasons, I felt that my husband needed more assurance from the Lord than ever.

After I thanked God for His love, I went into our living room. I told my husband about God's promise for his healing. Now, I did not tell my husband what scripture God told me for his healing, but I asked my husband to pray to God for the exact same scripture for confirmation.

I told my husband, "God revealed a scripture to me concerning your healing. I asked God to reveal the same scripture to you. In your prayer time, I want you to ask God to reveal it to you. I will continually ask God to give you the same scripture He gave to me."

Both of us prayed as we said we would. In my prayer time, I asked God to reveal the identical scripture to my husband, and my husband asked God to give to him the same scripture for confirmation.

Confirmation

A few days later, it was a Saturday morning; we were having coffee. I finished my coffee and walked into the kitchen to cook breakfast. My husband was still sitting at the breakfast table. My husband looked and said to me, "Hey, honey, I think I know what God said to you concerning my healing."

"Huh, what did He say?" I replied. My husband paused for a little while. He hesitated to say what he needed to say. I said, "Come on, spit it out. You know what He said." Then my husband used his finger knocker to start knocking on the table three times as he spoke, "I think…[knock] God said…[knock] For I am the Lord who heals you [knock]." With huge excitement, I said, "Exactly!"

Wow, he did not quote any other healing scripture but the *exact scripture* I received from God. By this, we knew for sure God spoke this word to us. We were filled with such joy. We knew it was a done deal. Spiritually, healing was a done deal. My husband just needed to go through physical treatment, that's all, but we knew spiritually, at that moment, his healing was done! We knew when God spoke that word to us, it was settled at that moment forever because God said it.

> Forever, O Lord, Your word is settled in heaven.
> (Psalm 119:89, NKJV)

> As the rain and the snow come down from heaven, and do not return to it without watering the earth and making it bud and flourish, so that it yields seed for the sower and bread for the eater, so is my word that goes out from my mouth: It will not return to me empty, but will accomplish what I desire and achieve the purpose for which I sent it.
> (Isaiah 55:10–11, NIV)

> For truly I say to you, until heaven and earth pass away, not the smallest letter or stroke shall pass from the Law until all is accomplished.
> (Matthew 5:18, NASB)

How wonderful are His promises? Every word that comes forth out of His mouth never will return to Him empty. It will accomplish what God has spoken.

Portland to Washington

My husband started the treatment and about two months into treatment, we needed to move to Oregon because he was hired by a company based in Portland. Well, we moved and settled in Portland. My husband was dealing with two major challenges. He had to learn about the new job as quickly as possible, which was demanding a lot of his attention, and he was dealing with the tremendous side effects from the chemo treatment.

I knew many nights he couldn't get any sleep because of the side effects. He went to work without having good rest. Every day, he was dealing with several medical side effects and his demanding client's requirements.

He went through eleven months of treatment. The result was devastating. Hepatitis C was still positive. He did not fully recover from this cancer. His doctor advised him to take care of himself better than before. If he did this, then my husband may live up to seventy years old without a lot of difficulties.

Well, he did not have any other choice at that time. He couldn't receive any more treatment because the chemo weakened his body and his immune system to dangerous levels. For hepatitis C, at that time, there was no other option. This treatment was the only option and could not be extended for safety reasons.

We did not understand why he didn't receive his healing. It could be because he was under the tremendous pressures of many things. We didn't understand the reason, but we still thanked God for His promise. We thanked God for my husband's healing. We thanked God for His faithfulness. We never doubted about His Word and promise. From time to time when we prayed, we just thanked God for the healing.

While we lived almost one year in Oregon, my husband found a new job, and we moved back to Washington. We moved back to the same town and attended the same church prior to moving to Oregon.

About five years later, during one Sunday morning service, our head pastor told the congregation that he has hepatitis C, and he was already under treatment for three months. He said his doctor told him that if he took care of himself, he can live up to seventy years old, but he decided to go under the treatment because he rather fight the cancer when he is younger rather than when he is seventy years old.

Second Attempt

Well, with that announcement, my husband realized the older he got, it would be more difficult to deal with cancer. So, he decided to go under the treatment for a second time. His doctor told him he had a very small chance of getting well—less than 5 percent—but he still decided for treatment by faith. The medications had been improved. He only had to give himself an injection once a week rather than four times a week in the previous treatment.

The doctor told my husband to give himself the shot on Friday evening, so he can rest through the weekend, but he was not able to rest even on weekend because he served the church. He served on Saturday nights and on Sunday morning. (Our church had Saturday night service and we were the head door greeters for Saturday).

Now, I am not telling you to do the same thing. I'm simple explaining it to you because we believed God's promises, and nothing was going to stop us from receiving our promise. We believed God's promise and were walking by faith. My husband volunteered in church more than before and traveled more than before for his work. Sure, he dealt with lots of side effects, but it didn't stop him.

It Is Done!

When he went in for the second treatment, I prayed to God for complete deliverance. I prayed, "God, your word says it is done deal."

> So when Jesus had received the sour wine, He said, "It is finished!" And bowing His head, He gave up His spirit.
> (John 19:30, NKJV)

> He himself bore our sins in his body on the cross, so that we might die to sins and live for righteousness; "by his wounds you have been healed."
> (1 Peter 2:24, NIV)

And I said to God, "There is no doubt in my mind and heart that when Jesus died on the cross he took all our sickness away. It is a done deal in the spiritual realm, but, Father, if it does not manifest in the physical realm, what does it mean to us? How does it benefit us? Father, if it fails again, I cannot see my husband go through this treatment a third time. So, Father, would you please once and for all, let your healing power manifest in his body? In Jesus name, amen."

This was my prayer for my husband every day. After six months of treatment, one day as I prayed, God told me, "It is done. You husband has beaten all those cancers cells. *It is finished.*" When I heard this from God, I knew it was finished. It was a done deal!

The next day, I asked my husband, "Have you been praying for your complete healing?" "Yes, I have." "Did God say anything to you?" Then my husband said, "I think. I've beaten it for good this time."

On October 27, 2006, Friday, we received final word from Dr. Alabaster. "The result is negative. No trace of hepatitis C." Hallelujah!

Merciful God

A few months later after my husband received his healing, God asked me a question. He asked, "During those seven years, before your husband received his healing, did you perfectly obey my words?"

"Huh?"

"Were you sinless while you were waiting to receive healing from me?"

"No, of course not, Lord?"

"If it was not your good deeds, then what caused you to receive an answer from me? Was it your prayer? Was it your fasting?"

I paused with this in my mind, *Huh, what does He mean?*

And He went on to say, "I know you believe in me, but that is not the only thing that caused you to receive an answer from me. During those seven years, you did not obey me completely and you were not sinless, but I still gave you what you wanted because I am merciful to you.

I didn't answer you because you had any good deeds. I answered you because you are my child, and because I love you, and because I promised to you that I would answer you." Then He revealed some wonderful scriptures to me.

> Not by works of righteousness which we have done, but according to *His mercy He saved us*, through the washing of regeneration and renewing of the Holy Spirit.
> (Titus 3:5, NKJV)

> But God, who is rich in mercy, because of His great love with which He loved us.
> (Ephesians 2:4, NKJV)

> For by *grace* you have been saved through faith, and that not of yourselves; *it is the gift of God, not of works*, lest anyone should boast.
> (Ephesians 2:8–9, NKJV)

> He who did not spare His own Son, but delivered Him up for us all, how shall He not with *Him also freely give us all things*?
> (Romans 8:32, NKJV)

As He revealed these scriptures to me, I realized I didn't receive healing from God because I was right during all those years. I didn't have any good deeds that would enable me to receive anything good from Him. During those years, I was not perfect. I received every good promise from Him because He loves me.

With this realization, I said, "Father, thank you so much for your love and tender mercies. You are right. My actions did not cause me to receive healing from you but only through your mercies and grace."

> "For we do not present our supplications before You because of our righteous deeds, *but because of Your great mercies*"
> (Daniel 9:18b, NKJV).

He Will Keep His Word

How long have you been waiting for your answer to manifest? Do you want to give up or want to complain? God wants me to encourage you by sharing this testimony. He wants you to know how faithful He is to His Word. He never changes His mind. He will keep His promises to you.

> Jesus Christ is the same yesterday, today, and forever.
> (Hebrews 13:8, NKJV)

> O Lord God of hosts, Who is mighty like You, O Lord? Your *faithfulness* also surrounds You.
> (Psalm 89:8, NKJV)

> He has remembered His mercy and His *faithfulness* to the house of Israel; All the ends of the earth have seen the salvation of our God.
> (Psalm 98:3, NKJV)

How long have you've been waiting for the manifestation of your miracle? It took us a total of seven years to receive our manifestation of healing. The first time, when my husband failed to receive healing, we didn't give up on praising God for His goodness and mercies. Though healing didn't manifest, we kept thanking God for the healing and praised God for His faithfulness. We never gave up our faith in God because we believed it was a done deal.

He loves to answer your prayers because you are His child. He promises to you in His Holy name. God wants you to have all hope in His Word and believe His Word. Because He loves you so much, God wants to answer your prayers more than you want to receive from Him. Just thank God for who He is in your life. Praise Him for His faithfulness to His Word. He will answer whatever you ask Him according to His Word.

Do you really believe He will answer you? You must believe He will answer you with all your heart because He will. Not because you are perfectly right with Him but because He is faithful and gracious to us all. Do you want to receive healing from God? Just know one thing, whether you believe it or not, healing is a done deal.

In the spiritual realm, healing is a done deal for you that was fully purchased at Calvary. Whether you believe healing or not, Jesus took stripes on His back for your healing. The only thing you need to do is thank God for it and receive it by faith.

He is faithful to His promises. Praise Him for His unchanging word. He has great mercies on all of us. We pray with faith, but ultimately, God answers our requests because *He loves us*. Amen.

> "In God, whose word I praise, In the Lord, whose word I praise."
> (Psalm 56:10, NASB)

> "I praise God for what he has promised; yes, I praise the Lord for what he has promised."
> (Psalm 56:10, NLT)

As God is alive, His word is alive. And His "Word" will prove to you, He is alive.

14

Witness to Sunny 1: Fortune-Teller

A lady moved into our community from another state, who I got to know. Her name is Sunny. When I was getting to know her, I asked if she was a Christian. She wasn't, but she was witness by many Christians. She told me church people prayed for her, even gave her a Bible and a hymnal, but she never made a commitment to Christ.

I noticed she had an interest in becoming a Christian, but for some reason, she was not ready to make that decision. I visited her from time to time in order to witness to her. I witnessed to her by sharing some of my personal testimonies of how I became a Christian.

As I shared my personal testimony to her, somehow, the Holy Spirit led me to share my experience of the fortune-teller story more than any other story. As you can tell from this book, I have many testimonies to share, but the Holy Spirit led me to share the fortune-teller story.

For me to share with you how I led Sunny to Christ by telling her about a fortune-teller I knew, I need to share with you what I'd shared with her.

A long time ago, before I became a Christian, I met this fortune-teller lady in South Korea. I had such a strange experience with this fortune-teller. What made my experience strange was that this fortune-teller recommended me to serve God. I was very surprised! I never expected a fortune-teller to witness to me about God. This fortune-teller talked to me more about God than any Christian I had ever met in my life! Isn't that strange!

Anyways, this fortune-teller had a little business in order to support herself. Her business was illegally buying and selling of American goods and trading it on the black market. At this time in Korea, if a person got caught doing this type of business, they would pay a huge fine and/or sometimes serve jail time too.

Now, because of her illegal business, she was very cautious about the people she met to do business. Whenever she met a new person to do business, she always asked that person's date of birth to figure out that individual's fortune. If that person fortune happened to not be good, she didn't do any business with that person, but if someone had been doing business with her for a while and she perceived their bad fortune, she warned them about their potential bad fortune in order to try to avoid big trouble.

I had some relationship with this fortune-teller. My friends and I visited her from time to time. Whenever she saw us, she habitually told us not only about our fortune but also witnessed to us about Christ too! She recommended for us to serve God!

I asked her why she suggested us to serve God and at the same time tell us of our fortune? She said, "One day, you and I will stand before God. Therefore, you must serve God as early as possible." This was so weird to me because I have a fortune-teller witnessing to me about God!

Also, one other odd thing was, she sent her own three children to the church. I asked her why she is sending her children to the church and she said, "They need to serve God because they are His creation." I can't serve God because of my situation, being a fortune-teller, but they must serve God as early as possible." This was also very strange to me at that time.

One day as usual, we gathered at her house. She, again, started telling us about our fortune, so I asked, "You said to me, I must serve God. Then why do you keep telling me about all my fortunes?"

"If I don't warn you about your bad fortune, how would you protect yourself from bad fortune. At least when I warn you, you would be more careful." Then she said, "I know God protects His people, but you're not His. Because you are not His, He won't protect you." Then she told me about her personal experience of how God protects His people.

This fortune-teller began to tell us a story that she experienced. She said that she knew a lady who did business with her some time ago. One day, she noticed this lady had such a bad fortune. That bad fortune could cause her to lose one of her legs. She knew for sure that this awful thing would happen to this lady.

She did not know how it would happen, but she knew for sure something awful would happen to this lady within a few months. Then when that very month came, instead of a terrible thing happening, she just had a minor incident.

This fortune-teller then told me she was very perplexed with this outcome. She knew for sure this lady was supposed to have such a bad fortune, but she could not figure out why it didn't happen! At first, she thought something happened to her psychic power—that something had gone wrong with her psychic power. Then she realized nothing was wrong with her psychic power.

She realized that the only reason a minor thing happened to this lady was because she was a child of Almighty God! She realized God's protection was over this lady. Over the time, this fortune-teller began to realize one thing—her accuracy of prediction always went wrong only with Christians.

She did not understand at first when it happened. She thought she lost her psychic power. But then she realized, her psychic power didn't work for Christians because God put His protection over His children.

Now, let me make myself very clear about her comment. You see, calamity does happen to the children of God. What she was simply saying, God protects His children from the worst situation. The point she was making was, if that lady was not a Christian, that lady's circumstance would've been far more worse than the minor incident she had.

After she shared this with me, she then told me this was the reason why she was telling me about my fortune. She said, "At least God protects His children but since you are not His child, I'm doing you a favor by telling you about your fortunes." I was not in the position to argue with her on any of her points, because at that time, I did not know God or the truth.

Then there were times this fortune-teller asked my friends and I not to be in the company with a lady who we all knew. Well, I am going to refer her as "Kim". The fortune-teller warned us to not be in company with Kim at all. Kim was a churchgoer. Well, Kim was supposedly a child of God as far as we knew.

Late one Sunday afternoon, we all gathered out in front of the small local convenient store. The fortune-teller called out and said, "She is a fake one!" With that loud shout, we all looked to see who she was referring to; she was referring to Kim!

We saw Kim from a distance. Kim was walking toward her apartment coming from church. We all saw Kim had her Bible and hymnal tuck inside of her arm. I asked the fortune-teller what she meant by "she is a fake one". Then she said to all of us, who were there, "Because someone goes to church, that doesn't mean they are a child of God. She is a fake one! She is not real!"

I have no way of knowing whether Kim is a fake Christian or not because I did not belong to God at that time, but for whatever reason, this fortune-teller must have known and could tell Kim was a fake Christian.

The fortune-teller kept warning us to not to hang out with Kim, a fake Christian. "Don't hang out with her. Don't do any business with her. She has a very bad fortune coming to her soon". Every time she saw us, she steadily warned us.

One day, I decided to ask what would happen if anyone would hang out with Kim. She explained, "If you happen to be with someone who supposed to have a bad fortune, you'll end up also receiving that bad fortune". I asked her to explain more.

"For instance, if you ride with her to go somewhere, and she happens to have a car accident, you also are involved in a car accident." It kind of made sense to me about her explanation. Then she continued, "Don't hang out with her because she definitely has a bad fortune." Well, I did not care one way other because I never did anything with Kim.

A few months went by and one morning, I had learned Kim was visited by the military police. The police stopped by her husband company to assist them in verifying whether the Hammer bowling balls that his wife purchased were for the black market.

You see, certain items sold inside of a military store were recorded and tracked by serial numbers to prevent black marketing, and the Hammer balling ball was one of those items.

In addition to this, at that time, once a year, the military commercial controls department selected people randomly to verify that the items they purchased with the serial numbers were still in their possession. How odd it was that Kim's husband's name popped up in random selection.

When the police got to her house, she couldn't provide the bowling balls to prove that she didn't sell them on the black market. She got caught! Just because of two small bowling balls, Kim's husband was kicked out of military service. He served the military for seventeen years. He was only a few short years away to retire from the military to receive a pension for the rest of his life.

All the benefits and retirement went out the window because the government discharged him from the military dishonorably. Just as this fortune-teller predicted the bad fortune of Kim, it happened to Kim as the fortune-teller had said. This fortune-teller was pretty accurate.

I also had a personal experience of my own with this fortune-teller and I shared it with Sunny. One day, this fortune-teller looked at me in the face and said, "You'll have an incident that will cause you to lose a huge sum of money. You'll soon have to let go of that money." Well, I didn't really care what she said because I tend not to believe in fortune-tellers.

From time to time when she saw me, she said the same things to me. "You'll have an incident that will cause you to lose a huge sum of money. You'll have to let go of that money."

So, I decided to ask her, "What incident? And when?"

She said, "During the month of May"

"The month of May? I know that! The month of May, I have to attend an event. My sister is getting married in May. I know I will have to let go of an abnormal sum of money for her wedding gift."

She went on, "No, not that. Your sister is not the one causing you to lose money. Someone else will."

"Someone? Who?" She didn't tell me who; maybe, she couldn't tell me who. I didn't pursue the answer because I brushed it off from my mind. I thought she could have mixed up her psychic information.

The month of May came and my husband and I and our children went to my mother's house to attend my sister's wedding. After the wedding, my sister went away for her honeymoon, all my immediate family gather together at my mother's house. Then all of a sudden, a huge argument broke out between my mother and my brother, and I got involved and pulled into the argument.

They were arguing about my brother living in my mother's place. She wanted him to move out, but at that time, my brother didn't have the means to move out. Nor did she have the means to help him move out. At that time, my husband and I were the only ones who had the means to help him out. So, we ended up helping him move out of my mother's place.

Well, just like the fortune-teller said, during the month of May, not my sister, but my brother caused me to spend a huge sum of money—nearly $1,800! It was lots of money back then. It was almost thirty years ago, and it is not a small amount nowadays too.

After I shared all these stories with Sunny, I told her I was quite surprised with this fortune-teller's accuracy. I told Sunny the more surprising thing to me was this fortune-teller, who predicted fortunes accurately, sent her children to church to serve God, witnessed to me about Almighty God, and recommended for me to serve God. I told her this fortune-teller acknowledged God and admitted that all of us will stand before God's judgment seat.

At that time, I didn't understand why I shared all those fortune-teller stories. About how this fortune-teller sent her children to the church, how God protects His children, and how fake Christians won't receive protection from God, and how this fortune-teller witnessed to me about God. I did not understand it at all!

I thought, I was just sharing to let Sunny know what experiences I had with the fortune-teller and how I became a Christian. A few weeks later, everything started to make sense to me. It all made sense why I shared more of the fortune-teller's story than any other story.

One day, when I visited her, she told me she had something to tell me. She was quite nervous. She said, "I know you don't know me and that you don't know anything about me, but it seems like you knew everything about me!" She continued, "I never shared my secrets to anyone because it embarrasses me so much, but whenever you talk about the fortune-teller, it seems you know all about me.

"I really need to tell you something. As you talked about the fortune-teller, I'll tell you that my mother is a fortune-teller too. My mother is heavily influenced by other spirits. As a matter of fact, my mother serves these spirits as her gods. My mother does not do anything without consulting with her gods. She won't do anything until she receives a sign through her dreams. I have kept this secret for a long time. It embarrasses me so deeply. I did not share it with anyone."

She continued, "I have been invited by many Christians to attend church, but I was afraid to go to the church. I heard that no one should serve two gods in one household. I heard if anyone accepted Jesus as Lord, then other gods (demons) get very upset and try to destroy that family. This was the reason I did not go to the church. I was fearful that the other gods might destroy my family."

"But your testimonies told me God protects His people. Your testimonies were telling me it is safe to serve God. You said God protects His people. If that fortune-teller told you to serve God, then God must be real, because I know other spirits are real. When I was a young child, I saw spirits in and out of my mom's house. I saw it. I know it is real."

I knew right there and then why I shared so much about the fortune-teller's story. This was the reason why the Holy Spirit led me to share about my personal experiences of the fortune-teller. It started to make sense to me. I was sent to her house to be a witness of Jesus Christ.

She asked, "What must I do? I am afraid. I do want to go the church. I do want to serve God, but I am afraid." I comforted her by sharing specific words of God with her. I encouraged her to accept Christ as her savior. I told her if she accepted Jesus as her savior, then no one or nothing can come against her to hurt her.

> "What then shall we say to these things? If God is for us, who can be against us?."
> (Romans 8:31, NKJV)

> I told her because Jesus is the "King of kings and Lord of lords"
> (Revelation 19:16, NKJV)

Everything must bow to Jesus including all *demons*.

> "That at the name of Jesus every knee should bow, of those in heaven, and of those on earth, and of those under the earth, and that every tongue should confess that Jesus Christ is Lord, to the glory of God the Father."
> (Philippians 2:10–11, NKJV)

I shared more scriptures to insured her that demons can't touch her.

> Then the seventy returned with joy, saying, "Lord, even the demons are subject to us in Your name."
> (Luke 10:17, NKJV)

> Once when we were going to the place of prayer, we were met by a slave girl who had a spirit by which she predicted the future. She earned a great deal of money for her owners by fortune-telling. This girl followed Paul and the rest of us, shouting, "These men are servants of the Most High God, who are telling you the way to be saved." She kept this up for many days. Finally, Paul became so troubled that he turned around and said to the spirit, "In the name of Jesus Christ I command you to come out of her!" At that moment the spirit left her.
>
> (Acts 16:15–18, NKJV)

I let her know that demons have no power to do anything to her if she has Christ living in her. I encouraged her by saying that she might even help her mother to be free from those demon spirits. She decided to accept Jesus as her savior. Halleluiah!

I took her to church with me every time I went until we moved to Oregon. And now she is a strong Christian. She still lives in the same city and the same state, Washington.

No harm ever came to any member of her family as she was worried about. Instead, a few years later, I ran into her at our local Costco parking lot and she told me her mother abandon other spirits and accepted Jesus Christ as her Lord and Savior too.

If you are reading this story, it is not by chance you are reading this. God led you to this book. He wants you know that the devil has no power over anyone's life in Christ. If you happen to know someone or you may be the one who is dealing with other spirit but afraid to come to God, don't worry about it. If you give yourself to God, God will make sure no one or nothing can even touch you or harm you. This includes any member of your family.

We know that anyone born of God does not continue to sin; the One who was born of God keeps them safe, and *the evil one (devil) cannot harm them.*

(1 John 5:18, NIV)

Behold, I give you the authority to trample on serpents and scorpions, and over all the power of the enemy, *and nothing shall by any means hurt you.*

(Luke 10:19, NKJV)

The Lord protects and preserves the they are counted among the blessed in the land—*he does not give them over to the desire of their foes.*

(Psalm 41:2, NIV)

Be free from other spirits. You must know that God loves you and cares for you deeply. If you repeat this simple prayer, God will come into your life and He will assist you in everything. Denounce that spirit and come to Jesus Christ. You will have a real life.

Will you repeat this?
Dear Jesus, I am a sinner.
    I repent of my sins. Please forgive me and save me
    by your shed Blood.
    Come into my life, I receive your gift of forgiveness.
    I open my heart to receive Jesus as my own personal Lord and Savior.
    In Jesus name I pray, amen.

"He who has the Son has life; he who does not have the Son of God does not have life."

(1 John 5:12, NKJV)

Denounce it right now and be free from it:

> "And right now, I denounce it in Jesus Name, all other spirits to leave out of my life. Right now, I am a child of almighty God and belong to Him. No one can touch me or harm me because God loves me. in Jesus name. Amen."

If you need help from others, please contact a local church pastor to assist you with this. May God Bless you with all His goodness for you for making this important decision.

> *As God is alive, His word is alive. And His "Word" will prove to you, He is alive.*

15

Witness to Sunny 2: I Was Watching You

Sunny started to come to church with me twice a week, Sunday and Wednesday. For Wednesday Bible study, I stopped by her house to pick her up. Now, as I wanted to seize any opportunity, I shared different kinds of my personal testimonies to encourage her to keep up with me for church. I did it because I had concerns she may drop out of coming to church before she meets Jesus.

After taking her to Bible study for three weeks, I told her that when a person accepted Jesus as their Lord, they are not only receiving salvation for their life, but they would also receive great financial blessings from God among other blessings. I told her this to encourage her and to pique her interest to keep coming to church to meet Jesus.

Lost Job

Well, what did I know? After I told her about God's financial blessing, a couple days later, my husband lost his job! "Now, what?" Well, I faced such a big dilemma. "What am I going to tell her?"

After all, she just started attending church. She doesn't know Jesus yet. She has not met Jesus yet to face this type of stumbling block.

I did not want her to be discouraged about God or think that God is not real because of our circumstance. I had great concern for her salvation. I wasn't worried about our financial situation because I knew God will take care of us, but I worried deeply about her salvation.

I knew, I needed to have some reasonable explanation for her why my husband, a child of God, lost his job. I knew, I was facing a huge spiritual battle. I needed to be very wise and fight this spiritual battle more for her than for ourselves. I needed to remain extraordinarily strong in the faith to prove to her God is absolutely real.

So, I prayed to God, "Father, give me wisdom and understanding. I need to let her know what happened to us. I can't hide it from her. She will eventually find out and will ask why this happened to a child of God. Father, I need your wisdom to answer her. Give me your understanding and wisdom."

The following week, I stopped by her house to pick her up for Bible study and I shared with her about our situation, but I told her we are not worried about it because God will give my husband a far better job than the one he lost. I told her, God will use this bad situation as a stepping stone to bless us even more financially and told her, He will use this adverse situation to bring more blessing to us.

Even in the midst of our big spiritual battle, I said many positive things in order to encourage her. Three weeks had passed and finally, just as I expected, she asked, "How come your husband lost his job? Didn't you tell me God takes care of His own? You are a child of God. Could God not prevent your husband from losing his job? Could He not?" Wow, I knew eventually she would ask this question and she did!

I explained it to her with God's wisdom. "Believers or non-believers, we all are affected by natural laws and circumstances. Christians can and do lose jobs just as non-Christians, but we overcome it in a very different way. We have God who is always ready to help us in time of need.

We have all His promises. Non-Christians have no promises from God. They must depend on the natural realm to help them, but we have a supernatural realm from God to help us. God knows everything about our situation. He will help us in an amazing way.

You will see how God helps my husband to find a far better job than the one he had before. You watch and see how God will take care of His children. He will do it as He promises because God is alive." This was my explanations to her, and she heard every bit of it.

I knew, I had a huge responsibility in my hands. I must and needed to make sure I receive the answer from God; otherwise, every testimony about God could turn out to be nothing to her. She might wind up believing there is no God.

So, during my prayer time, I prayed this, "Father, I do not want her to think that you do not exist and that you are not real because of our circumstance. I do not want our situation to be a stumbling block for her to get to know you. I know who you are, and I know you are for sure, but she doesn't know you. She doesn't even know you exist.

"I am asking you to answer our prayers not for us but for her. Don't delay in answering for my husband new job; otherwise, she will doubt you. She doesn't know you. She doesn't know whether you are real or not. You must and need to answer our prayer as quickly as possible for her sake."

After I prayed, I praised God for who He is and what He can do. I said, "Father, I know who you are. You are almighty who created the heaven and earth. There is nothing impossible for you because you are the God of all flesh. I know you will bring a far better job for my husband."

I continually picked her up for Wednesday Bible study. It ended around noon, which was lunchtime. Since we both had to have a lunch, she and I always stop by one of the Korean restaurants to have a quick bite to eat. At that time, the lunch special was $4.99 per person, and with a tip, for two persons, the meal would cost about $12.

I always paid for the meal. I did that for two reasons. One, I didn't want her to think that I was afraid to spend money, because I didn't believe God would supply all our needs. And two, I didn't want her to have a wrong perception about God's existence and my faith because I feared to spend money.

She did offer to pay for the meal occasionally, but I insisted to pay for all lunches. I paid all the lunches and picked her up until we moved to Oregon, which was more than twelve weeks of Wednesday Bible studies.

I prayed for her salvation about two weeks then God shined His light on this scripture:

> And He said to them, "Which of you shall have a friend, and go to him at midnight and say to him, 'Friend, lend me three loaves; for a friend of mine has come to me on his journey, and I have nothing to set before him'; and he will answer from within and say, 'Do not trouble me; the door is now shut, and my children are with me in bed; I cannot rise and give to you'? I say to you, though he will not rise and give to him because he is his friend, yet because of his persistence he will rise and give him as many as he needs."
>
> (Luke 11:5–8, NKJV)

Then God also led me to this:

> I am the bread of life. Your fathers ate the manna in the wilderness and are dead. This is the bread which comes down from heaven, that one may eat of it and not die. I am the living bread which came down from heaven. If anyone eats of this bread, he will live forever; and the bread that I shall give is My flesh, which I shall give for the life of the world.
>
> (John 6:48–51, NKJV)

God showed me a few things in these verses. He helped me relate these verses to the characters as Sunny and I. God revealed,

Sunny is my friend who came to me from a long exhausting journey of life, and I, the friend, who went out at midnight to ask bread for my friend.

God revealed these scriptures to me, so I would pray with understanding of His love for her. I was so delighted and strengthened to pray for her salvation because I knew God revealed these scriptures to me for His good purpose.

I applied Luke 11:5–8 in my prayer. "God, I am asking you for the bread of life for my friend Sunny. She came to me from a long journey of her life. I do not have bread to give to her, but you do. Father, give your bread of life to her. Without the bread of life, she will die forever."

I prayed fervently for her salvation daily. I didn't have any doubt that God would answer my prayer. I knew that God would give His bread of life to Sunny because He promises to answer any prayer if I pray according to His will.

> This is good and acceptable in the sight of God our Savior, who desires *all men to be saved* and to come to the knowledge of the truth.
> (1 Timothy 2:3–4, NKJV)

> Now this is the confidence that we have in Him, that if we ask anything *according to His will*, He hears us.
> (1 John 5:14, NKJV)

I continually prayed the bread of life for her and for my husband's new job. "Father, I am not asking you to answer our prayer of a job for us but more for her. I know that you are real, and I know you will take care of us. I do not have any doubts about you, but she doesn't know you yet."

"She doesn't know that you truly exist. I do not want her to think that you are not real because of our circumstance. I do not want our situation to become a stumbling block for her to get to know you. You must and need to answer our prayer as quickly as possible for her sake."

Those prayers were going on for nearly three months. One day, Sunny and I were coming home from Bible study, she asked me to stop by her place to have a cup of coffee. As we were having coffee, she said, "You amazed me. Last week, I told my husband I could not believe what I am witnessing. I told my husband *God must be real!*"

When she told me this, I immediately had a sense of victory! I sense the triumphant! Then I immediately heard the Holy Spirit, "YOUR HUSBAND GOT THE JOB!" With this voice, I knew for sure my husband and I won the victory. We won one of the hugest spiritual battles we faced!

She continued, "Every week, you came to pick me up for Bible study, I was expecting to see something different from you, like worrying or crying. As each week passed by, I didn't see you worrying nor heard you crying.

Then I said to myself, 'Maybe next week she will cry, maybe next week she will show worry and stress.' But then the following week came, you were the same as the previous weeks! You are consistently the same throughout the whole time. I didn't see any changes from you."

She continued, "I remembered when my husband lost his job when we were living in Hawaii. After a month has passed and he did not find a job, I began to worry so much. I thought, I would lose my mind. I was so afraid that my husband may not find a job for a long time. I worried so much I couldn't sleep or eat.

When I finally broke down and couldn't take it anymore, I suggested to my husband that I would take our children with me to go to our home country to stay with my mother, and he should move in his sister place in Washington until he finds a job. I told him to give me a call when he finds a job.

Two months of waiting for my husband to find a new job was so torturing for me. It was way too long for me to wait and way too much for me to handle. It's been nearly three months for you, but I couldn't see any fret or worry from you. Instead, you are always happier than ever."

Wow, I could sum up everything she said in one phrase. "I was watching you the whole time!" She was watching me the whole time! Just as I told her, "You watch and see." She had watched whether or not I would hold on to my confession of faith. She was observing my faith. Then I received a huge revelation from God! God brought us together for His good purpose.

> "And we know that all things work together for good to those who love God, to those who are the called according to His purpose."
> (Romans 8:28, NKJV)

For me, because of her, I needed to stay strong with my faith and confession. If she was not in my life at that time, I do not know how I would have handled the situation, or what I would have said about the stressful situation, but because of her, I had to fight the good fight of faith.

Because of her, I was more determined to prove God is indisputably real. I was determined to make sure my situation would not discourage her to meet Jesus Christ. Because of her, I stayed focus in my belief and confession. She was in my life to prove and strengthening my faith.

For Sunny, my testimony of faith perked her interest to know God. Through the witness of my faith, as she mentioned, "*God must be real.*" She really wanted to find out whether God is real or not for herself and I was in her life to prove that God is undeniably real!

After we moved to Oregon, she kept going to church by herself. Then she finally had a personal experience with God to realize God is unquestionably real. As I mentioned in the first story of Sunny, she remained strong in Christ, even to this day. She serves Christ with all the love from her heart. God worked everything good for His purpose for me and for her.

After having coffee with her that day, I went home. As I was opening my front door, my husband greeted me at door. When I saw him, I said, "You got the job!" He looked perplexed with my statement. He asked, "How do you know?"

"I know you got a job. We won the spiritual battle."

"How do you know?"

I explained it to him what had happened at Sunny's house and told him we triumphed. My husband couldn't understand it, but he didn't question it either.

A few days later, one morning, God prompted my husband to contact one of the companies he did the final interview. He kind of gave up this company because they didn't contact my husband for nearly three weeks. When my husband made the call, they said they did make a decision to hire him, but they forget to call him, and on that call they offered him a job!

Now, no one knows why they forget to call him or how long they forget to call him. Nevertheless, whatever the reason was, God worked a miracle for us.

I personally believed God did something mighty for us when I heard God said, "Your husband got the job!" I give all the glory to God because I know God prompted my husband to make that call, and God helped them to make a decision to hire my husband on that call. This was how my husband received his second job from God. Though we needed to move to Oregon, we gave all thanks to God. Hallelujah!

Now, most of us know someone who needs to receive salvation. I want to encourage you not to give up on prayer for someone's salvation. You may think that you have been praying for someone's salvation for a long time, and it seems like it is taking God a very long time to answer. Don't get discouraged. Instead, you should have the full confidence and joy of praying for someone's salvation because you are praying according to the will of God.

You see, God wants to give everyone the bread of life. God's words tell us that. Ask God for the bread of life for your love ones. He will give your love ones the bread of life as He promised in His Word.

> "For God did not send His Son into the world to condemn the world, but that the world through Him might be saved."
>
> (John 3:17, NKJV)

Now, if you are going through a hard time while you are witnessing to someone, put your focus onto others instead of focusing on your bad situation. I know it is not easy to do that, but although you may be going through some tough times, if you put other's matter before yours, God will honor your faith.

Besides, if you truly believe God will take care of you, you should not worry about your situation. You should know that God knows what you are going through. Have faith in God. He knows all about your situation. Therefore, He will take care of you.

Keeping on being a witness of Jesus Christ. Don't give up on witnessing of Jesus because you are going through a hard time. If God sees, you are willing to put others' eternal salvation before your situation, God will honor you because of your love for others. Your rewards will be great! Keep on witnessing to the one who don't have "the Bread of Life".

Witness to lost souls not only with words but also with action. Always be mindful about the one who you are witnessing; they are watching you. Just like Sunny watched me. They are observing your confession and faith in Jesus Christ. Don't be a mere talker of faith. You must be a walker of faith. Fight the good fight of faith through action and love. God, who sees, you are testifying Jesus Christ through faith action, will reward you greatly.

You will be in for a big surprise to discover that the one you are witnessing to is in your life for God's good purpose. Just as Sunny was in my life for God's good purpose. As I explained it to you, her purpose for me was so I could hold on to my confession and faith through action.

Remain faithful to God. God does everything for His good perfect reason and for your good. Understand why that person is in your life. Ask God to help you to understand.

> "And we know that all things work together for good to those who love God, to those who are the called according to His purpose."
> (Romans 8:28, NKJV)

Ask God to give you wisdom, understanding, and strength. He will give all you need to testify Jesus Christ. God will prove through you that Jesus Christ is undeniably real. He will not cause you to fail in your testimony about the Lord Jesus Christ. He will use you to prove that Jesus Christ is unquestionably real and alive. Just tell God whatever concerns you have.

Ask God for whatever your needs from Him to prove Jesus Christ is real in your life. Ask Him! He will give you all your needs for His purpose. He will equip you to prove that Jesus is absolutely real and alive through you. Remember, God uses all believers to reveal that Jesus Christ is real to all mankind. Ask! He will give it to you to become a real witness of Jesus Christ.

> "Ask, and it will be given to you; seek, and you will find; knock, and it will be opened to you."
> (Matthew 7:7, NKJV)

May the God of love strengthen you with all His powers and love!

As God is alive, His word is alive. And His "Word" will prove to you, He is alive.

16

Witness to Sunny 3: God Stopped Demon's Power

We moved to Oregon and lived there for about eleven months before returning to Washington in the same city we had left. A couple of years later, I ran into Sunny in the Costco parking lot. She was so excited to tell me about her personal testimony.

She said, "After you moved to Oregon, I had an amazing experience. I truly experienced that God is alive!" She went on, "After you moved, my husband and I wanted to buy a house, but we were short on the amount we needed for a down payment. So, we decided to ask my mother to loan us some money, but I had one great concern.

"My mother does not do anything without receiving a sign from her gods. She typically receives signs through her dreams, and she only does what her god tells her to do. I know my mother very well. I witnessed that she even would not do what my father wanted because she received a sign from her god.

I was concerned that she would not loan any money to me if her god tells her not to do so. But though I had this concern, I still decided to ask her anyway to loan us the money, and I took that concern to God. I decided to copy your style of prayers and prayed exactly what I wanted. Do you know what I did?"

"What?" I asked.

"I prayed for God to prevent my mom from having any dreams! I asked God to stop her from having any dream, so she would loan us the money we needed to purchase our home. Well, a few days had passed and I decided to give my mom a call and asked what she decided to do.

She said, she didn't know what to do. She had been praying and waiting to have a dream, but somehow, she couldn't have any dreams! I knew why she couldn't have any dream! God had prevented her to have any dreams. My mother said, 'Well, I really don't know what to do, but I guess, I need to loan you the money.' And with that remark, I insisted that my mother loan us the money as soon as possible for our down payment.

How amazing it is! God answered my prayer! Now I know for sure He is real. Not only because of your testimonies, but now from my own personal experience. He is real, and He is alive!" I was very happy for Sunny because she finally knew that God is real.

It was through dreams that her mother learned what she must to do for certain situations; however, concerning about loaning money to Sunny, she couldn't have any dreams. Well, what she didn't know was that God is the most powerful Spirit being able to stop other spirits from giving her any dreams. What she didn't know was, if our God decides to prevent her from having any dreams, she couldn't have any dreams. What she didn't know was when our God stepped in, demons have no power to do anything. They become totally powerless and useless.

The Bible talks about how demons do have some power to perform some signs, but once God is involved, their power is destroyed, and they can do nothing.

God's Mighty Powers

You could see this from the book of Exodus when God sent Moses and Aaron to Pharaoh to release the children of Israel from Egypt. Moses let pharaoh know this request was coming from God, but Pharaoh didn't believe it and demanded some proof.

> "When Pharaoh speaks to you, saying, 'Show a miracle for yourselves,' then you shall say to Aaron, 'Take your rod and cast it before Pharaoh, and let it become a serpent'."
>
> (Exodus 7:9, NKJV)

As Aaron threw the rod down, it changed into a serpent, but Pharaoh did not care because his magicians could do the same thing.

> But Pharaoh also called the wise men and the sorcerers; so the magicians of Egypt, they also did in like manner with their enchantments. For every man threw down his rod, and they became serpents. But Aaron's rod swallowed up their rods.
>
> (Exodus 7:11–12, NKJV)

Because his magicians had some power to perform such miracles, this caused Pharaoh not to care nor have any fear of God. But the important fact Pharaoh failed to realize was that the snake from Aaron's rod swallowed the snakes from his magicians' rods. This was the key reason why Pharaoh made a big mistake and received the wraths of God that brought catastrophe to his nation.

> Then the Lord spoke to Moses, "Say to Aaron, 'Take your rod and stretch out your hand over the waters of Egypt, over their streams, over their rivers, over their ponds, and over all their pools of water, that they may become blood. And there shall be blood throughout all the land of Egypt, both in buckets of wood and pitchers of stone.'"… Then the magicians of Egypt did so with their enchantments; and Pharaoh's heart grew hard, and he did not heed them, as the Lord had said.
>
> (Exodus 7:19, 22; NKJV)

> So Aaron stretched out his hand over the waters of Egypt, and the frogs came up and covered the land of Egypt. And the magicians did so with their enchantments and brought up frogs on the land of Egypt.
>
> (Exodus 8:6–7, NKJV)

Pharaoh hardened his heart because Pharaoh's magicians were able to do the same thing. Pharaoh couldn't differentiate between God's power and the power from his magicians, but once God decided to intervene, Pharaoh's magicians could not perform any miracles. You are able to see this from next set of scriptures.

> And they did so. For Aaron stretched out his hand with his rod and struck the dust of the earth, and it became lice on man and beast. All the dust of the land became lice throughout all the land of Egypt. Now the magicians so worked with their enchantments to bring forth lice, *but they could not*. So there were lice on man and beast. Then the magicians said to Pharaoh, "This is the finger of God." But Pharaoh's heart grew hard, and he did not heed them, just as the Lord had said.
>
> (Exodus 8:17–19, NJKV)

Pharaoh's magician clearly lets him know that this was the work of God. Pharaoh magicians couldn't perform any miracles. They performed miracles only to the point God allowed them to do so. Once God said, "Enough", once God "Stepped in", they couldn't do anything. Pharaoh's magicians became useless and powerless.

From this event, every disaster happened to Egypt by God's power, they couldn't prevent it from happening or perform anything. (Please read Exodus 8–12). They couldn't do anything for Pharaoh, and they couldn't do anything to prevent disaster from destroying their land. They just stood and watched everything that took place by the hand of Almighty God.

Let's look at one more scripture:

In the book of Acts, there was a slave girl who had a demon spirit.

> Now it happened, as we went to prayer, that a certain slave girl possessed with a spirit of divination met us, who brought her masters much profit by fortune-telling. This girl followed Paul and us, and cried out, saying, "These men are the servants of the Most High God, who proclaim to us the way of salvation." And this she did for many days. But Paul, greatly annoyed, turned and said to the spirit, "I command you in the name of Jesus Christ to come out of her." *And he came out that very hour.* But when her masters saw that their hope of profit was gone, they seized Paul and Silas and dragged them into the marketplace to the authorities.
>
> (Acts16:16–19, NKJV)

This demon spirit helped her to predict the future for her owner. Her owner was greatly benefitted by her fortune-telling but when Paul rebuked the spirit out of her, she could no longer tell fortunes for her owner. She no longer had ability to predicts fortune. (Read Acts 16:16–23).

This evil spirit only did what it did because God let it. Once again, God decided to step in, and this spirit became powerless. Not only was it not able to do anything, demons recognized, acknowledge and announce that God is the most high God and is the most powerful Spirit being because demons know who God is.

> "She followed Paul and the rest of us, shouting, 'These men are servants of the Most High God, who are telling you the way to be saved'."
>
> (Acts 16:17, NIV)

Throughout the entire Bible, God talks about demons and their power. God let all of us know there are demon spirits and their power, but God also let us know their power completely gets destroyed when God steps in.

That was the reason why Sunny's mother couldn't have any dreams. Demon spirits could not show anything to Sunny's mom as before because God stepped in and prevented them in order to bless Sunny. (Please read 1 King 18:16–40. It will help you to understand even more about God's power.)

> *Therefore you will no longer see false visions or practice divination.* I will save my people from your hands. And then you will know that I am the Lord.
> (Ezekiel 13:23, NIV)

> Now the night will close around you, *cutting off all your visions. Darkness will cover you, putting an end to your predictions.* The sun will set for you prophets, and your day will come to an end.
> (Micah 3:6, NLT)

Demons are real, as you know, and they can perform some signs, *but* they cannot do anything to God's people, because God protects His people.

> We know that whoever is born of God does not sin; but he who has been born of God keeps himself, and the *wicked one does not touch him.*
> (1 John 5:18, NKJV)

> There is no divination against Jacob (you), no evil omens against Israel (Your nation or your house whole). It will now be said of Jacob and of Israel, 'See what God has done!'
> (Numbers 23:23, NIV)

You see, there is no divination nor evil omens that can work to hurt God's people. You must not be fearful of it because it cannot do anything to God's people. God destroyed its powers, God demolished it powers.

> "And having disarmed the powers and authorities, he made a public spectacle of them, triumphing over them by the cross."
> (Colossians 2:15, NIV)

What a wonderful testimony Sunny had. God, by stopping the demon spirit, answered Sunny's prayer to give her what she wanted. These demons that operated in her mother's life were completely stripped of their power to do anything. Now, she truly has her own personal testimony about God and His power. She has her own testimony to let others know God is real and alive.

After meeting her at Costco, a couple years had passed and I ran into her again at Costco. She had an even more beautiful testimony to share with me. Her mother and sister accepted Jesus Christ as their savior and denounced all other demonic spirits forever and received the promise of eternal life. Halleluiah! What a testimony!

One last thing I would like to mention to you is that if you are involved with the wrong spirits like Sunny's mom, please return to God! God is waiting for you. You don't have to be bound by these evil spirits. God loves you and is ready to help you. I strongly encourage you to "denounce it" like Sunny's mom by repeating this prayer of inviting Jesus into your life and go to a local church to seek help from them. They will help you anyway they can.

> Dear Jesus,
>> I am a sinner.
>> I repent of my sins.
>> Please forgive me and save me by your shed blood;
>> Come into my heart.
>> I receive you as my own personal Lord and Savior. In Jesus's name.

Denounce it right now: He is beside you to help you. God will take care of you.

> "And right now, I denounce it in Jesus name, all other spirits to leave out of my life. Right now, I am a child of Almighty God and I belong to Him. No one can touch me or harm me because God loves me and protects me in Jesus name. Amen."

Because you denounce that spirit and accepted Jesus as your "Lord and Savior", you now have a real life and promise of a new beginning and eternal life.

> "He who has the Son has life; he who does not have the Son of God does not have life."
> (1 John 5:12, NKJV)

> *As God is alive, His word is alive. And His "Word" will prove to you, He is alive.*

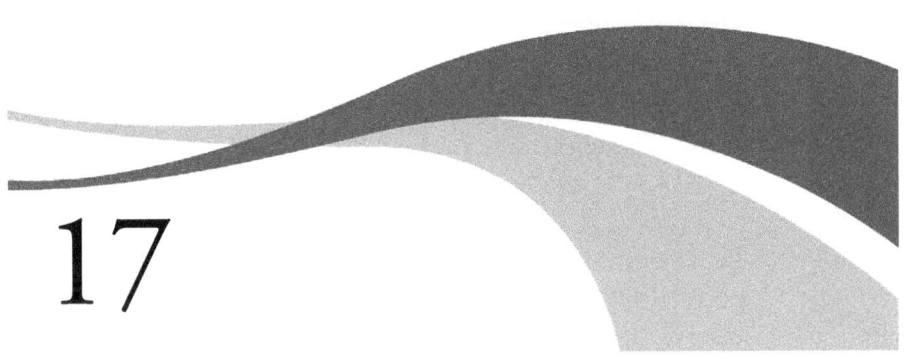

17

Second Job: You Can Do It Again

We were devastated and restless when my husband lost his first civilian job. We realized it wasn't going to be easy to a find a job that pays as well as the first one. His first job was nothing but a 100 percent miracle from God. Without any civilian job experience, without any marketing experience, there was nothing we could have done to receive that miracle. God brought that miracle for my husband. It was done for us because God orchestrated that miracles for us.

Now, when my husband was looking for his second job, we faced three major spiritual battles. A new job, healing for my husband's hepatitis C, and Sunny's salvation. For my husband's healing from hepatitis C, God gave Exodus. 15:26, "For I am the Lord who heals you," as a faith seed to plant in our heart.

For Sunny's salvation, God wanted me to use the reference of Luke 11:5–8 and John 6:48–51 as a seed faith to pray for her. But for my husband's new job, I didn't have any particular scripture as a faith seed to plant in my heart. So, I just used the same scriptures from the first job's prayer as faith seeds to pray for his second job.

And my God shall supply all your needs according to His riches in glory in Christ Jesus.
(Philippians 4:19, NKJV)

Be anxious for nothing, but in everything by prayer and supplication with thanksgiving let your requests be made know to God.
(Philippians 4:6, NKJV)

In the same way God, desiring even more to show to the heirs of the promise the unchangeableness of His purpose, interposed with an oath. In order that by two unchangeable things, which it is impossible for God to lie, we may have strong encouragement, we who have fled for refuge in laying hold of the hope set before us.
(Hebrews 6:17–18, NKJV)

For I, the Lord, do not change; therefore you, O sons of Jacob, are not consumed.
(Malachi 3:6, NKJV)

"Bring whole tithe into the storehouse, so that there may be food in My house, and test Me now in this", saying the Lord of hosts, "if I will not open for you the windows of heaven, and pour out for you a blessing until it overflows."
(Malachi 3:10, NASB)

For as many as may be the promises of God, in Him they are yes; wherefore also by Him is our Amen to the glory of God through us.
(2 Corinthians 1:20, NKJV)

No Faith Seeds

I did believe that God would show us His mercy and kindness toward us to find a good job like he did with the first one, but I believed God would answer my prayers of needing a job more because of Sunny. As you may know from Sunny 2 story, I prayed to God to answer our prayer of a job as quickly as possible because of her.

I told God, I didn't want her to doubt about His existence because of our situation. I believed God didn't want Sunny to doubt Him, and remain as an unbeliever because of our situation too. Therefore I, convincingly, believed that God would answer our prayers quickly because of her sake. Well, basically, I was banking on God's answer for us because of her.

And other than using the scriptures above as faith seeds and banking on His answer on our situation because of Sunny, I didn't have any scripture reference to believe God would bring a good job as the first one. I didn't have a strong conviction that my husband would find a job that paid as good as the first job.

The reason I didn't have a strong conviction was, my husband's new resume was not much different from the first job search resume. He only had a little more than one-year experience in marketing; it was practically the same as the first resume. It didn't have much to offer like the first resume.

I knew, since my husband's resume was no different from the original one, we really needed God's miracle to find a good job like the previous one. We really needed His miracles to find a job that pays well as the first one.

Consequently, I had deep concern—concern that His miracle might not happen for us a second time. *What if God's miracles doesn't happen to us like the first one, then what?* I did brush off these thoughts, but I still felt very uneasy about our second job's prayer request.

> "Will the Lord reject forever and never again show favor? Has His faithful love ceased forever? Is His promise at an end for all generations? Has God forgotten to be gracious? Has He in anger withheld His compassion?" Selah
> (Psalm 77:7–9, HCSB)

Just like the psalmist, I had similar concerns. "In His anger, is He going to withhold His Miracle?" "Is He not going to do one more miracle?" "Will He do miracles again?" "What if He doesn't? Then what must we do?" "What must my husband do?" I was not sure whether God would do a miracle twice in the same situation.

Though my husband didn't say this to me, from time to time, I could see he worried about the same thing. I felt, I really needed more faith seed as substances and evidence to believe that God will do one more miracle for us.

> "Now faith is the substance of things hoped for, the evidence of things not seen"
> (Hebrews 11:1, NKJV).

Remember

I still prayed to God every day for a new job. As I was praying for a job, one day, the Holy Spirit reminded me of some particular scriptures! He reminded me how God asked the Israelites to remember what He had done for them! So, I found a few scriptures and began to read.

> And *remember* that you were a slave in the land of Egypt, and the Lord your God brought you out from there by a mighty hand and by an outstretched arm; therefore, the Lord your God commanded you to keep the Sabbath day.
> (Deuteronomy 5:15, NKJV)

> You shall not be afraid of them, *but you shall remember well* what the Lord your God did to Pharaoh and to all Egypt.
> (Deuteronomy 7:18, NKJV)

> *Remember* His marvelous works which He has done, His wonders, and the judgments of His mouth.
> (Psalm 105:5, NKJV)

> *Remember* the former things of old, For I am God, and there is no other; I am God, and there is none like Me.
> (Isaiah 46:9 NKJV)

As I began to meditate on these scriptures, suddenly, it dawned on me! Just as God asked the Israelites to remember what He had done for them, He was asking me to remember what He had done for our life! All of a sudden, I remembered all the mighty miracles He had done for our life! I went back to memory lane of ours answered prayers.

Then I said, "God, I remember what you've done for our life. You healed my husband's chronic asthma. You healed my back problem. I remember how you sold our house in Texas. I remember how you brought my husband's first civilian's job. Father, I remember all the marvelous works and wonders you did for our lives. All these were done for us because you love us and care for us."

I went back in memory lane to remind myself and to thank God for what he had done for us, just as the psalmist said.

> And I said, "This is my anguish; But I will remember the years of the right hand of the Most High."
> I will remember the works of the Lord; Surely I will remember Your wonders of old. I will also meditate on all Your work, And talk of Your deeds.
> (Psalm 77:10–12, NKJV)

In the midst of my own anguish—anguish of doubting if His miracles would not be done for us anymore—I remembered and meditated on what He had done for us. His wonders of my past days. I exalted His mighty power and love for us.

Then all of a sudden it dawned on me that He can do miracles for us again. So, I confessed, "*Father, I know you can do it again!* You created the whole universe from nothing. You are the owner of the whole universe, and since nothing is too difficult for you, *you can do it again*. You are the God of all flesh and there is no one like you. You are the owner of all things; Nothing is impossible for you. Father, I know *you can do* another miracle for us again! Because you are real God."

> "Ah, Sovereign Lord, you have made the heavens and the earth by your great power and outstretched arm. Nothing is too hard for you."
> (Jeremiah 32:17, NIV)

Wow. How good our God is. He is loving and amazing. How can any words describe who He is? No words can describe Him! I gave all the praise, honor, and glory to Him for what He had done in our life and what He will continue to do in our life. Now, I had substance and evidence to believe He would do more miracles for us, just as He did for us in the past. The anguish I felt began to finally evaporate.

Every morning when I prayed, I thanked God for what He had done in our life and what He is going to do for us in the future. I thanked God for all His answers. I thanked Him for His faithfulness. I thanked Him for His unchanging love. I thanked God for all the miracles He performed in our life.

My memories went back to past years to remember how God answers were evident in our life. And I exalted Him for His mighty powers. I prayed liked this for a few days.

Do You Really Believe?

One day, as I was praying, I meditated and remembered His miracles and thanking God for what He had done for our lives. All of a sudden, the Holy Spirit reminded me of the event of the Wall of Jericho and the crossing of the Red Sea, and He asked, "Do you really believe the miracle of the wall of Jericho?"

"???"

"Do you really believe the miracle of the dividing of the Red Sea?"

"???" I never thought about it until He asked me these questions. After these questions, I paused for a moment to think about it and asked that question to myself. "Do I really believe in those miracles?" Then I realized, I do really believe in the miracle of Jericho and the Red Sea! There were no doubts in my mind about those miracles! I truly and truly believed it happened as God said it happened.

Then instantly I confessed, "Father, when the walls of Jericho fell, I was not there, but I truly believe you did it. I know for sure you caused it to fall. Father, I wasn't there when you divided the Red Sea, but I know for sure you divided it. Even though I wasn't there to see with my own eyes, I know you brought down the walls of Jericho, and you divided the Red Sea."

"Father, comparing to what you did at Jericho and at the Red Sea, bringing another job for my husband is nothing to you. It is a very small miracle for you to do. It is a very simple miracle for you to do compared to those miracles. In Jesus's name, I truly believe you'll do another miracle for us again."

> You will see neither wind nor rain, says the Lord, but this valley will be filled with water. You will have plenty for yourselves and your cattle and other animals. *But this is only a simple thing for the Lord*, for he will make you victorious over the army of Moab!
>
> (2 Kings 3:17–18, NLT)

> Behold, I am the Lord, the God of all flesh; *is anything too difficult for Me?*"
> (Jeremiah 32:27, NASB)

Assurance

I knew right at that moment, God would answer our prayer for the second job not because of Sunny's sake but for our sake. Right there and then, I knew for sure God would bring us a job that pays just as good as first job or even better. I knew compared to what He did at Jericho and the Red Sea, bringing a wonderful job for my husband is a very simple miracle for God to do! I knew then He would do another miracle to take us upward.

Wow, what a wonderful Counselor we have. We were battling three huge spiritual battles. It was not easy for me to stay firm in the faith for all three. But with the help of Holy Spirit, the spiritual battle becomes far easier for me to believe all things will be done for us.

I gave all the praise to God. God knew what I needed. I needed more than a few scriptures to reinforce my faith. During this difficult time, I needed to boost up my faith to believe that God will bring another miracle for us.

The Wonderful Counselor inside me led me to the events that happened in the Bible to help me boost up my faith. He helped me to understand that bringing a new job to my husband is a very simple miracle for God to do. I thanked God for His Spirit who guided me into the perfect will of God to pray for our needs.

After this revelation, I had strong assurance that God would do another miracle for us and deliver us. Now I had more faith substance and evidence to know God would do a miracle for us.

New Understanding

Let's see something here as God showed me. Through this experience, I discovered another amazing understanding of the Bible.

Until this point, I didn't know I could use Bible's miracles as my prayer references. You see, the descendants of Israel did not see the miracles that God did for their ancestors. They only heard of it from their forefathers, just like you and I heard it.

> How great you are, Sovereign Lord! There is no one like you, and there is no God but you, *as we have heard with our own ears.*
> (2 Samuel 7:22, NIV)

> *Things we have heard and known, things our ancestors have told us.*
> (Psalm 78:3, NIV)

> *We have heard with our ears*, O God, Our fathers have told us, The deeds You did in their days, In days of old: You drove out the nations with Your hand, But them You planted; You afflicted the peoples, and cast them out. For they did not gain possession of the land by their own sword, Nor did their own arm save them; But it was Your right hand, Your arm, and the light of Your countenance, Because You favored them.
> (Psalm 44:1–3, NKJV)

They only heard God's miracles from their ancestors. They never saw it, but they never doubt what they heard. Throughout the Bible, the descendants of Jacob put faith in God from what they heard and not what they saw, and they use what they heard as references to make supplication and petitions before God.

For example, in Psalms 106, the psalmist never saw what took place for his forefathers. He had knowledge of what had happened based upon what he heard, but he referred to the entire historical event to praise God and make petition to God for deliverance of their situation. He made his petition based upon what he heard and not based on what he saw.

> Remember me, O Lord, with the favor You have toward Your people. Oh, *visit me with Your salvation*... Many times He delivered them; But they rebelled in their counsel, And were brought low for their iniquity. Nevertheless He regarded their affliction, When He heard their cry; And for their sake He remembered His covenant, And relented according to the multitude of His mercies. He also made them to be pitied By all those who carried them away captive. *Save us, O Lord our God*, And gather us from among the Gentiles, To give thanks to Your holy name, To triumph in Your praise.
> (Psalm 106:4, 43–47, NKJV)

Moses was not there when God made a covenant with his forefathers—Abraham, Isaac, and Jacob—but Moses also made petition before God for forgiveness of the sins of Israel according to what he heard from his forefathers.

> Remember your servants Abraham, Isaac, and Jacob. You bound yourself with an oath to them, saying, "I will make your descendants as numerous as the stars of heaven. And I will give them all of this land that I have promised to your descendants, and they will possess it forever." So the Lord changed his mind about the terrible disaster he had threatened to bring on his people.
> (Exodus 32:13–14, NLT)

How about Daniel? The prophet Daniel prayed according to the promise God made to the prophet Jeremiah of freeing Israel from Babylon. Daniel didn't hear it with his own ears, but He believed what he read in the scriptures and prayed based on this.

> For thus says the Lord: After seventy years are completed at Babylon, I will visit you and perform My good word toward you and cause you to return to this place.
>
> (Jeremiah 29:10, NKJV)

> In the first year of his reign I, Daniel, understood by the books the number of the years specified by the word of the Lord through Jeremiah the prophet, that He would accomplish seventy years in the desolations of Jerusalem.
>
> (Daniel 9:2, NKJV)

Let's look at one more example: The prophet Daniel and three of his companions—Shadrach, Meshach, and Abednego—were taken to Babylon as captives, but whenever Daniel made prayer to God, he prayed toward Jerusalem, toward the temple that Solomon built, according to what Solomon prayed to God. (For more information, please read 1 Kings 8–9:9)

> And if they have a change of heart in the land where they are held captive, and repent and plead with you in the land of their captors and say, "We have sinned, we have done wrong, we have acted wickedly"; and if they turn back to you with all their heart and soul in the land of their enemies who took them captive, and *pray to you toward the land you gave their ancestors, toward the city you have chosen and the temple I have built for your Name*; then from heaven, your dwelling place, hear their prayer and their plea, and uphold their cause.
>
> (1 Kings 8:47–49, NIV)

> Now when Daniel learned that the decree had been published, he went home to his upstairs room where the *windows opened toward Jerusalem.* Three times a day he got down on his knees and prayed, giving thanks to his God, just as he had done before.
>
> (Daniel 6:10, NIV)

Throughout the Bible, you will find many situations of how the descendants of Israel use their forefathers' testimonies or promises as a reference to make petitions to God. The descendants of the Israelis did not see any miracle of God with their eyes. They didn't hear them with their own ears about the covenant God made with their forefather, but they accepted and believed what they've heard from their forefathers.

They did not doubt what they were told by their ancestors. And still to this day, the people of Israel believe all the miracles and promises of God and use it as a reference to make petitions to God.

Let' think about something here also. When God created the universe, you and I were not here yet, but we fully believe that God created all of it; therefore, why can't you believe His miracles that are recorded in Bible?

How did you get saved? Just like salvation, you and I were not there when Jesus was born. You and I were not there when Jesus died on the cross, and we were not there when He ascended to heaven, but because we accepted and believed what God said about Jesus and our salvation, we received His assurance of eternal life.

> "Though you have not seen him, you love him; and even though you do not see him now, you believe in him and are filled with an inexpressible and glorious joy."
>
> (1 Peter 1:8, NIV)

This is the same as you and I not being there when the walls of Jericho fell. We weren't there when the Red Sea was divided. So, we should do like now day Israelis. They were not there when those miracles took place, but they believe every miracle recorded in the Bible. They do not doubt it!

Why should you doubt? Do you doubt because you are not a natural Israeli? According to Bible, you and I are adopted to Him as natural Israelis. Therefore, you have all the rights and privileges, as a natural Israeli to receive all the goodness and promises from God.

> "And if you are Christ's, then you are Abraham's seed, and heirs according to the promise."
> (Galatians 3:29, NKJV)

Now, you may not have any personal miracles to reference, but you can use the miracles recorded in the Bible to make petitions to God, just like I did. Use it as reference to let God know how you believe all those miracles happened in the Bible. Believe it and use it as a reference for your faith, like I did, like the Israelis did.

Let God know, you believe a mighty miracle will happen to you just as it was done in the Bible. I believe all the Bible miracles without seeing it. Why should you doubt? You must believe God that God will bring a miracle for you just as He did for me and for Israel.

> Jesus said to him, "Thomas, because you have seen Me, you have believed. Blessed are those who have not seen and yet have believed."
> (John 20:29, NKJV)

> Jesus said to her, "Did I not say to you that if you would believe you would see the glory of God?"
> (John 11:40, NKJV)

Can I ask you same questions that God asked me?

> "Do you really believe the miracle the of Jericho?"
> (Joshua 6:1–27)

> "Do you really believe the miracle of the Red Sea?"
>
> (Exodus 14:1–31)

> "Do you really believe the miracles of the leper receiving healing?"
>
> (Matthew 8:1–4)

> "Do you really believe the miracle of raising a dead girl back to life and the healing the woman with the issue of blood?"
>
> (Matthew 9:18–26)

> "Do you really believe miracle that Jesus healed the Blind and the Mute?"
>
> (Matthew 9:27–33)

Do you? Do you really believe? If your answer is "unsure", then ask God to help you to believe. God will help you to overcome your unbelief. God doesn't want you to pretend to believe. He rather you to be truthful to Him like this father below. And choose to believe because Jesus said, "Everything is possible for one who believes."

> Jesus asked the boy's father, "How long has he been like this?" "From childhood," he answered. "It has often thrown him into fire or water to kill him. But if you can do anything, take pity on us and help us." "If you can?" said Jesus. Immediately the boy's father exclaimed, *"I do believe; help me overcome my unbelief!"*
>
> (Mark 9:21–24, NIV)

Believe and confess it with your mouth what you believe then you'll see His glory.

For with the heart one believes unto righteousness, and with the mouth confession is made unto salvation.
(Romans 10:10, NKJV)

Then He touched their eyes, saying, "According to your faith let it be to you."
(Matthew 9:29, NKJV)

Jesus said to him, "If you can believe, all things are possible to him who believes."
(Mark 9:23, NKJV)

As God is alive, His word is alive. And His "Word" will prove to you, He is alive.

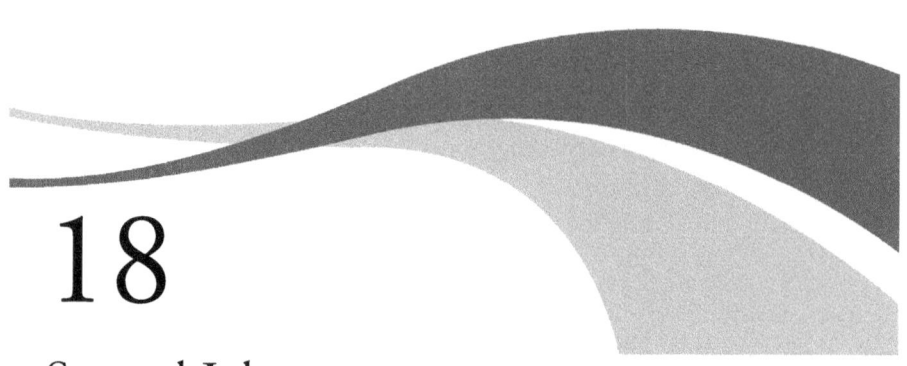

18

Second Job: Don't Block Your Answers!

This testimony happened when I first met Sunny. At that time, everything was coming at us all at once. My husband lost his job, discovered he has hepatitis C, and I met Sunny with the task of witnessing to her about Jesus Christ. Three major actions were happening to us at the same time. My husband and I realized, it was not going to be an easy spiritual battle for us.

Once again, the only one we had for sure was God, His mercy, love, and unchanging promises. Three major prayers were going on at the same time—my husband's healing, him needing a new job, and for Sunny's salvation.

My husband and I wrote down faith scriptures, meditated on these scriptures, and prayed. We prayed together and individually. For my husband's job prayer, every time I prayed, Holy Spirit often reminded me about Daniel's twenty-one days of praying.

> "But the prince of the kingdom of Persia withstood me twenty-one days; and behold, Michael, one of the chief princes, came to help me, for I had been left alone there with the kings of Persia."
> (Daniel 10:13, NKJV)

"Prince of the kingdom of Persia" here indicates the kingdom of evil spirits. This spirit prevented the archangel Gabriel from delivering God's message to Daniel; therefore, the archangel Michael had to come to help Gabriel to delivered God's message to Daniel.

The Holy spirit kept reminding me how Daniel's prayers were prevented by the evil spirits. I understood what had happened to Daniel's prayer, but while Holy Spirit reminded me of Daniel's prayers, I couldn't make any connection with my prayers for a new job. I was wondering what this scripture meant to my prayers? *Do the evil spirts block our answer?* Well, I didn't receive further revelation about it, but my prayers for a new job continued.

So Many of Interviews

When my husband looked for his first civilian job after he retired from the military, he didn't receive any calls for an interview for nearly three months. Not even a single call. Literally, at the end of the third month, he received a call and was invited to only one interview, and that's how my husband received the blessing of a job.

However, this time was very different from the first time. In a week, interviews were requested by two to three different companies. My husband was invited to interview after interview. Some companies even payed for all the travel expenses for my husband to fly to do final interview in another city. God kept my husband very, very busy with so many interviews.

These many interviews gave us high hopes and expectations that God would answer our prayers soon. We expected God would help my husband find a job very quickly, but as time passed by, nothing was happening. High hopes and expectations began to wear out.

Hope because some other companies asked him for an interview. Disappointment because previous companies that interviewed him called and gave him bad news. Hope and disappointment were repeated every week. We felt like we were on a roller coaster. Week by week, disappointment of not finding a job grew worst. It made both of us spiritually very tired.

I could see my husband's exhaustion. He had more of a burden than me to carry because he was the main bread earner. He was pressured to find a job as soon as possible, but nothing was happening.

In addition to looking for a job, my husband had to deal with the side effects of the hepatitis C chemo treatment. At that time, he was on treatment about two months. This treatment had such a negative impact on his appetite, sleep, and pain in all of his joints. The lack of appetite changed his appearance as he lost a great deal of weight and was losing hair on his head and eyebrows.

Both situations took such a toll on him. It was way too much for him to deal with, especially the side effects of the treatments, and the constant hope and disappointments of finding a new job. Though it was very stressful to us, we both remained faithful to God. We put all of our trust and hope in God.

Hopes and disappointments, as a riding roller coaster, had been going on for nearly three full months. Once and for all, I needed to understand about my prayers. I needed to understand why I didn't get an answer for my husband's job situation. It was very weird for both of us.

My husband was called in for final rounds of interviews so many times but none of them resulted in a new job. With that many interviews, my husband already should have gotten a job! But he didn't! Besides, God promised me that He will do another miracle for us to find a job, as the first job, but nothing seemed to be happening.

I set down and sought after God. I needed to find out, once and for all, what is going on with our job searching! "Father, I don't understand all of this. Your word says you are full of compassion and love. You say you will not break a bruised reed nor put out a smoldering wick."

> "A bruised reed he will not break, and a smoldering wick he will not snuff out. In faithfulness he will bring forth justice."
> (Isaiah 42:3, NIV)

"Look at my husband! Look at him, God! He is like a bruised reed and a smoldering wick. Where is your compassion? Where is your goodness? How come you haven't done anything for him? How come? I don't understand all of this? Didn't you say you are full of compassion? Where is your compassion? Where is your kindness and goodness?" After I said this, God answered me immediately with this!

> "Do I take any pleasure in the death of the wicked?" This is the declaration of the Lord God. "Instead, don't I take pleasure when he turns from his ways and lives? For I take no pleasure in anyone's death." This is the declaration of the Lord God. *So repent and live!*"
> (Ezekiel 18:23, 32; HCSB)

When I heard this from God, I knew instantly my husband had not dealt with his transgressions. Whatever transgression it was, I didn't know, he had not repented of it. I just received a revelation from God why our prayers were hindered. It was hindered by unrepented sins. Of course, unrepented sins block anyone's prayer from being answered!

After I heard this from God, I gathered my Bible, hymnal, and went to the living room. I look at my husband and said, "I just asked God that I don't understand about God's compassion on your job situation. I told God that you looked like a bruised reed and fainting wick, and I could not see any of His compassion on you. I challenged God's compassion, His goodness, and kindness. Then this is what He said to me." I quoted Ezekiel 18:23 and 32 to my husband.

The moment I stopped quoting the scripture God had given me, I saw my husband's face. His face looked as white as snow. It got so paled, and I saw deep convictions on his face. He didn't say anything to me but got up from the floor, where he was sitting, grabbed his Bible, hymnal, and walked into our bedroom.

He shut the door behind him and was in that room for more than an hour. When he came out of the room, I didn't ask him anything, but I knew it had to do with "sin and repentance". I didn't know what his sins were, but whatever sin it was, it must have been settled in that room!

After this incident, about a week later, I went to the living room after my prayer. My husband looked at me and said, "I got the job."

"You got the job? How? I didn't hear the phone ring?"

"Well, I called them when you were praying."

"You called them, where?"

"In Oregon."

"In the state of Oregon? What prompted you to give them a call?"

"Well, they told me they would give me call the following weeks. I know, it's nearly been three weeks. I thought about it, and instead of assuming they didn't want me, I decided to give them a call. "When I called, the hiring manager was very apologetic because they made the decision to bring me on but forget to give me a call."

"Forget to give you a call?"

"Yes, I am so glad I gave them a call, but if I accept their offer, we have to move to Oregon."

"Well, if we have to move, then we have to move." Hallelujah!

As I shared this with you in Sunny story 2, God did reveal to me at Sunny's house that my husband got the job. Spiritually, I already knew he got the job. I just didn't know where he would get the job, but after my husband told me what had happened, we knew this was the job God revealed.

We decided to accept the job and moved to Oregon. We moved, but we didn't want to live there too long. We wanted God to bring us back to the same city we were living in. We decided to trust God to bring us back within a short period of time.

As we wanted to come back to Seattle, God brought us back to the same place that same year. In January of that year, we moved to Oregon, and we moved back to Seattle in the month of November, eleven months later.

A few months later, while my husband was working at his new job in Oregon, he told me what happened in our bedroom that day. He said, "When you told me about Ezekiel 18:23, 32, I knew exactly what God was talking about. When I went to the bedroom, I sat before God and repented of my sins."

"What sins?"

"Well, when you mentioned Ezekiel, I knew right there and then, I had not forgiven those people who let me go and hurt me from my job. I thought, I had forgiven them, but deep down inside my heart, I didn't forgive them. I still held bitterness and anger against them. I held on to the offenses because it hurt me so much."

"I said I forgave them, but I kind of wanted to see some vengeance for myself. I knew it was wrong to hold on to these offenses, but I had a very hard time letting it go and forgiving them."

My husband continued, "I prayed to God to have mercy on my situation, but I wanted them punished for what they did wrong too. Oftentimes, I focused on what they did to me, I couldn't see the real me for myself. I couldn't see my mistakes, my disobediences, my wrongs, and my unbelief. I acted on many situations out of fear, doubts, and anger rather than faith and love. I contributed a great deal into that situation, but I refused to acknowledge my part and wrongdoing.

"Moreover, I felt God's justice was very unfair to me. From my point of view, they were not good and very unfair towards me, but somehow, I got let go from my job instead of them. When I went into the room and began to have a truthful conversation with God, I began to see and acknowledged my faults, my mistakes, and my sins in many areas."

"God wanted me to acknowledge my faults, my strongholds, and my weakness, but not theirs. My stronghold and weakness are the biggest stumbling block for me to receive God's best blessing for my life. God knew if I didn't acknowledge this weakness in me, I would run into a similar situation again and again. It was not their fault. It was all my fault."

> "Have you not done this to yourself by your forsaking the Lord your God When He led you in the way?."
>
> (Jeremiah 2:17, NASB)

"What I realized is this, God used that bad circumstance for me to see myself accurately and to teach me to improved myself. So, when I do run into a similar situation in the future, I would not react the same way as before to receive the same results. God helped me to see myself, so I wouldn't make the same mistake allowing Satan to steal God's blessing from us."

Wow, what a great revelation he received about himself! That day, my husband finally acknowledged all his faults and forgave them all. Just as my husband admitted, oftentimes we tend to blame God or others for our bad situation, but how we reacted toward the situation, negative reactions, cause bad things to happen to our life.

We gave all the praise to God! His grace was shone upon my husband to see "the truth" about himself and set him free from all the hurts and all the deceptions of Satan.

When God revealed Ezekiel to me, I knew his unrepentance of transgression hinder our answers from God, but I didn't know what it was. Satan was working overtime on my husband. Satan wanted to make sure my husband wouldn't forgive those people. Satan wanted to keep my husband under his territories, bondages, and control.

He kept reminding my husband what they did to him and how wrong they were to him. By reminding my husband of all these hurts, it prevented my husband to see the truth, it prevented my husband to see his own faults, and "the Prince of the kingdom of Persia" prevented our prayer from being answered for nearly three full months.

Satan knows unforgiveness is one of the great sins that blocks God's answers.

Unforgiveness blocks God's blessing from coming to anyone's life. Satan knows it very well. So, Satan works very hard to keep reminding us what others did wrong to us. How they did wrong to us, but it doesn't matter what others did and how hurtful they were to us, we must forgive and trust God for justice.

Unforgiveness is one of the greatest sins that bound believers, and it definitely blocks God's answers from coming to us.

> Your wickedness has deprived you of these wonderful blessings. *Your sin* has robbed you of all these good things.
>
> (Jeremiah 5:25, NLT)

Indeed, the Lord's hand is not too short to save, and His ear is not too deaf to hear. But your iniquities have built barriers between you and your God, and *your sins* have made Him hide His face from you so that He does not listen. For your hands are defiled with blood (unrepented sins) and your fingers, with iniquity; your lips have spoken lies, and your tongues mutter injustice. (Blaming everyone except you)
(Isaiah 59:1–3, HCSB)

When you lift up your hands in prayer, I will refuse to look at you; even if you offer countless prayers, I will not listen. Your hands are covered with blood (sins).
(Isaiah 1:15, HCSB)

If anyone refused to forgive and hold on to an offense, Satan is reigning over their life. Anyone that hold on to an offence and doesn't let it go, Satan is taking full advantage of their life.

"Now whom you forgive anything, I also forgive. For if indeed I have forgiven anything, I have forgiven that one for your sakes in the presence of Christ, *lest Satan should take advantage of us*; for we are not ignorant of his devices"
(2 Corinthians 2:10–11, NKJV)

Unforgiveness is one of the clever scheme of Satan! If Satan keeps reminding you of what others did wrong, he is doing it for a good reason. As you just read, unforgiveness causes Satan to take full advantage of your life. Through unforgiveness, Satan blinds your eye to see the truth—the truth about yourself, the truth about your mistake, the truth about your faults, the truth about your unbelief, and the truth about your weakness.

These are the reasons why Satan keeps reminding you of what others did wrong; to keep you in bondages of its influences, and through unforgiveness, Satan prevents your prayers from getting answered!

> "Be alert and of sober mind. Your enemy the devil prowls around like a roaring lion looking for someone to devour."
> (1 Peter 5:8, NIV)

There are many who are deceived! "The prince of the kingdom of Persia," Satan, works through bitterness, anger, greed, wrong motives, etc. All these things Satan uses against believers to prevent them from receiving all the good things from God. Get rid of it. It's not worth it! It is not worth a penny. All the sins are not worth keeping.

It is a scheme of Satan! It only causes you to have a bad relationship with God. It is only there to hurt you and rob you of God's blessing. Satan is not concerned about your well-being. God is the only one who is truly concerned about your well-being. Let it go! Don't block your answer! It is not worth it!

> So My heavenly Father also will do to you if each of you, from his heart, does not forgive his brother his trespasses.
> (Matthew 18:35, NKJV)

> For if you forgive men their trespasses, your heavenly Father will also forgive you.
> (Matthew 6:14, NKJV)

> For judgment is without mercy to the one who has shown no mercy. Mercy triumphs over judgment.
> (James 2:13, NKJV)

> Now whom you forgive anything, I also forgive. For if indeed I have forgiven anything, I have forgiven that one for your sakes in the presence of Christ, *lest Satan should take advantage of us*; for we are not ignorant of his devices.
> (2 Corinthians 2:10–11, NKJV)

You know, God is the God of all gods and God of all flesh. Therefore, nothing is impossible for God to do. God has all the power to give you what you've been asking. Just as in the blink of eye, God can change the entire circumstances in one second, but oftentimes, unrepented sins block God's blessing from coming into our lives. Let it go!

> For the Lord your God is God of gods and Lord of lords, the great God, mighty and awesome, who shows no partiality and accepts no bribes.
> (Deuteronomy 10:17, NIV)

> God will bring this about in His own time. He is the blessed and only Sovereign, the King of kings, and the Lord of lords.
> (1 Timothy 6:15, HCSB)

> Ah, Sovereign Lord, you have made the heavens and the earth by your great power and outstretched arm. Nothing is too hard for you.
> (Jeremiah 32:17, NIV)

> I am the Lord, the God of all mankind. Is anything too hard for me?
> (Jeremiah 32:27, NIV)

Let go of any offenses! Don't let Satan deceive you one second more. Don't let Satan rob you of what's rightfully yours in Jesus's name! Don't let the prince of the kingdom of Persia block your answer. Check your heart deeply to see what is in it and let it go. Do not give the devil a foothold in your life.

> "In your anger do not sin. Do not let the sun go down while you are still angry, and do not give the devil a foothold."
> (Ephesians 4:26–27, NIV)

God knows how it hurts you. He knows how much it hurts you. But although it is hurting so much, if you are willing to let it go, His power will come to strengthen you. If God sees you are willing to let it go, His power will strengthen you faster than you can imagine. His power will come to you like a lightning bolt.

If you need help, ask the Holy Spirit to help you. I know when the pain is so deep, it is not easy to let it go, but you can do it through His power. The Holy Spirit is sent to strengthen you to obey His Word. Let it go. God knows man's willpower is weak and limited. This is one of the main reasons why God sent the Holy Spirit to us, to strengthen us and to carry out God's will and help us to be free from Satan's oppression.

> "I can do all things through Christ who strengthens me."
> (Philippians 4:13, KJV)

You must know this for sure that God loves you dearly. He loves you more than anything else. He loves to help you. He wants to help you quickly. He wants to answer you quickly. He wants to deliver you quickly. Just "don't let unforgiveness cost you and your relationship with God. Don't let unforgiveness block your answers from God." In Jesus's name.

> Your wickedness has deprived you of these wonderful blessings. Your sin has robbed you of all these good things.
> (Jeremiah 5:25, NLT)

When you lift up your hands in prayer, I will refuse to look at you; even if you offer countless prayers, I will not listen. Your hands are covered with blood (sins).

(Isaiah 1:15, HCSB)

As God is alive, His word is alive. And His "Word" will prove to you, He is alive.

19

Are You Perfect?

A few years after I became a child of God, I struggled to believe that I was righteous by the blood of Jesus. I began to have the thought that I didn't deserved to be His child. I read my Bible many times and learned what pleases God and what doesn't, and I tried my best to live my life according to His Word, but just like Paul cried out in Romans 7:15, I realized I don't do what I should do, but I do more what I shouldn't do.

For example, whenever I had an argument with my husband.

> "In your anger do not sin. Do not let the sun go down while you are still angry."
> (Ephesians 4:26, NIV)

I knew very well what this scripture meant, but I let the sun goes down and remained in anger. I knew, I am supposed to let go of anger as soon as possible and forgive, but I didn't. Often, I remained in anger for a few days or until we reconciled instead of letting it go.

And again:

> Therefore if you bring your gift to the altar, and there remember that your brother has something against you, leave your gift there before the altar, and go your way. First be reconciled to your brother, and then come and offer your gift.
> (Matthew 5:23–24, NKJV)

I knew this scripture very well too regardless who was at fault. I still had a responsibility to settle any issues before I went to His altar to pray, but because I didn't practice what I knew, it hindered me from praying and reading the Bible.

This could take a few days. I stopped my spiritual devotion until I reconciled the issues. Then I resumed reading my Bible and praying. This pattern was repeated so many times and so often.

This began to affect my spiritual life. It made me feel like I am unworthy to be His child because I refused to practice the Word, refused to submit to the Word of God. I didn't do what I should do, but I did do more of what I shouldn't do.

I knew I was justified by faith and not by works (Romans 4:28), but I could not shake these thoughts and feelings of unworthiness. Many thoughts ran through my mind, "I should not have disobeyed God. I have known God for many years. It is not like I met God yesterday. I've known Him for a while."

"I know who He is and what He has done in my life. I have experienced so many of His miracles, but why am I acting like I don't know Him? I know Him. What is wrong with me? Why am I having a hard time obeying Him?"

These kinds of thoughts continually tortured me. I felt condemned and unworthy. I was in fear that God may not love me anymore. I did confess my sins of disobedience, but I still felt so ashamed of myself.

Though I felt so ashamed of myself and lost all confidence to pray, I still prayed every day to meet my obligations. But when I prayed, I prayed as though I was unworthy to pray. What I mean is,

I prayed to God with so many shameful emotions. This feeling was there for about three months. "Shame, shame, and shame."

One day, when I was praying, God allowed me to see myself in a vision. I saw myself sitting on the floor praying but in a very odd posture! My face was turned to the left side, and I lifted my jacket to cover the right side of my face, despite never wearing a jacket when I prayed.

I realized, I saw myself in this odd position trying to hide myself from God. I hid my face because I was so ashamed to look straight toward God, like Adam and Eve in the garden (Genesis 3:8).

Immediately after this vision, God asked me a question. "Are you raising perfect children?"

I replied to Him, "No."

He asked another question, "How many times did you correct them for the same thing?"

I replied, "I'm still correcting them up to this day."

"Do you still want to have a relationship with them?"

"Of course, God!"

"Why? Why do want to have a relationship with them? Don't you get tired of telling them the same thing repeatedly?"

"Yea? but I still want to have a relationship with them."

He then asked me, "Why?"

I thought to myself with a dumbfound expression, *What? Why is He asking all of these questions?* So, I respond to Him with a little bit of confusion, "What are you saying, Father? Although they don't listen to me all the time, because they are my children, I still want to have a lifetime relationship with them."

"Besides, I still need to tell them repeatedly in order to teach them about life, faith, and many other things that I've learned. In this way, they can minimize their mistakes and the pain they will experience in life!"

Then He said to me, "SO DO I. I am also raising tons of imperfect children who repeatedly disobey me just as your children. You said, although they are not listening and imperfect, you still want to have a lifetime relationship with them. Then what makes you think that I don't want same thing with you?"

Then I said, "Oh my god!" Up to that instant, I did not understand why God asked all these questions. He knew all along that I was struggling from my disobedience. He knew all along I was ashamed of myself for being disobedient. He knew, I was under condemnation.

Then He asked me another question, "Do you want your children to be ashamed of themselves because they disobeyed you? Do you want them to hide from you because they felt ashamed of themselves? Do you want your children to walk around with their shoulders drooping and their heads held down because they felt bad about themselves? Are you happy when they can't even look at you straight because of shame?"

When He asked all these questions, I couldn't say a word to Him except I said, "Oh my god."

"Do you want your children to accept your forgiveness and move on with their lives without being ashamed? Do you want them to understand your love for them? Do you want them to live their life with your love and support even though they didn't obey you? Do you want them to come in and out of the house confidently?"

I didn't know what to say to Him. The only thing I said to Him was, "Of course, God. Of course, God. I do not want them to be ashamed of themselves. I do not want them to think they are not worthy of themselves. I want them to learn from their mistakes and move on with their life with my love and support. I do not want them to be disappointed in themselves. I want them to accept my forgiveness and have all the confidence they can have."

Then God said, "SO DO I. This is the exact thing I want for my imperfect children." Then He said to me, "I don't want you to be ashamed of yourself even when you disobeyed me. I know your mistakes and disobediences. I just want you to be honest with me and be yourself. Just admit it to me. I have already forgiven you. You just need to accept my forgiveness and move on with your life with my love and my support."

Then He led me to this wonderful scripture to set me free from all self-condemnation. And told me, "You are perfected in my love."

> 15 Whoever confesses that Jesus is the Son of God, God abides in him, and he in God. 16 We have come to know and have believed the love which God has for us. God is love, and the one who abides in love abides in God, and God abides in him. 17 *By this*, love is perfected with us, so that we may have confidence in the day of judgment; because as He is, so also are we in this world. 18 There is no fear in love; but perfect love casts out fear, because fear involves punishment, and the one who fears is not perfected in love.
>
> (1 John 4:15–18, NASB)

Let's understand what God is saying, in verse 15, if you acknowledge that Jesus is the son of God and accept Him as Lord and Savior, then God abide in you and you in God. Verse 16 says, "God is love, and the one who abides in love abides in God, and God abides in him." And if you are abiding in God, you are abiding in His love! Do you understand this? If you abide in God, you are abiding in God's love because God is love!

Verse 17 says, "By this, Love is perfected with us."

"By this," God is in you and you in God, His "love" is perfected with you. Just simply accept and believe that you are in God and God in you, His love made you perfect! Not what you did or will do that makes you perfect! Because you are His child, His love has made you perfect.

My big mistake was, I tried to be perfected through my obedience instead of relying on His love. I didn't know this, I am already perfected in His love, not because what I did or will do, just because I am a child of God, I am already perfected in Him! Hallelujah!

Verse 18 says, "There is no fear in love. But perfected love casts out fear, because fear involves punishment, and the one who fears is not in perfected love." I was in fear of punishment. I feared that God does not love me anymore. I thought, I was cut off from His love because I disobeyed. I feared and felt ashamed of myself because I did not understand I am perfected in His love. And that perfected love cast out fear of punishment.

I had experienced this with my children. When they did something wrong, they avoided me from fear of punishment. If I tried to engage them in conversation, they wanted to keep it very brief for fear of punishment, but what they fail to understand is, just as I failed to understand, I have already forgiven them. I just want them to be honest with me and to themselves.

There is no fear of punishment because Jesus paid the price for our punishment. Praise God! Just like you raised imperfect children, God revealed to me, He is also raising tons of imperfect children. It does not matter how many times your child disobeys you, or make mistakes, your love for them never changes. You may get angry at them for a moment and dislike what they did for a moment, but you don't hold resentment toward them forever. And you want them to know and be sure of this.

You do not want your children to doubt your love for them because they made a mistake. God is quick to forgive, and He doesn't want you to ever doubt His love for you because you made a mistake. God may disapprove what you did, but He will not hold it against you at all.

Our children will make mistakes, but we continually forgive them. We will make mistake, but God will continually forgive us. Our children will make mistakes, but we continually love them just as God continually loves us. We know, we cannot earn His forgiveness or love. You are a child of God. He loves you just as you are.

If you failed to submit to the word of God as I did, you have a wonderful Savior who died for your sins. Just confess it to Him. He knows it before you even admit it to Him. God says just confess it to Him. He promised He would forgive, if you confess it to Him.

You won't have any special feelings when you confess your sins. You just need to believe and accept His forgiveness. Tell Him everything that's bothering you. Whatever it is, He already knows it. He just wants you to be honest with Him. He knows everything about you. Just admit it to Him and believe and accept His forgiveness.

You are justified not by works but by faith. Therefore, believe He forgave you.

> If we confess our sins, He is faithful and just to forgive us our sins and to cleanse us from all unrighteousness.
> (1 John 1:9, NKJV)

> Therefore, having been justified by faith, we have peace with God through our Lord Jesus Christ.
> (Romans 5:1, NKJV)

Let's think about something here. What if you told your child you have forgiven him, but he doesn't believe you? What if he walks around with shame and guilt all day or for many days because he doesn't believe you? What would you do? You may tell him again and again that you have forgiven him. But what if he continually believes you did not forgive him, how would you convince him you already did? Would you not want your child to believe what you said and accept it and be free from guilt and condemnation? Free from fear of punishment?

In the same way, you need to believe God's words and accept His forgiveness because God has forgiven you! Don't make the same mistake as I did! I repented of my sins every day but failed to accept His forgiveness and allowed the devil to torment me. God doesn't want any of His children to live in fear and doubt of His forgiveness. If you are struggling with condemnation, would you please admit it to God that you failed to accept His forgiveness?

You became a child of God, not because of anything you did, but because of everything Jesus Christ did. You can't be perfected through your works, but through all the work Jesus Christ has done for you.

God also revealed to me one more important thing. He said if I try to be perfected and righteous through my works, then I am literally cutting myself off from Christ and will eventually fall out of His grace.

> "For if you are trying to make yourselves right with God by keeping the law, you have been cut off from Christ! You have fallen away from God's grace."
>
> (Galatians 5:4, NLT)

God revealed, if I don't become fully dependent on what Jesus did for me to make me righteous, then Jesus will not have anything to do with me at all. Don't try to be perfect and righteous through your works. You will be cut off from Christ and fall away from His amazing grace.

> Yet we know that a person is made right with God by faith in Jesus Christ, not by obeying the law. And we have believed in Christ Jesus, so that we might be made right with God because of our faith in Christ, not because we have obeyed the law. For no one will ever be made right with God by obeying the law.
>
> (Galatians 2:16, NLT)

No one can be perfected and righteous by their works. No one, this includes you and me. You are only perfected in and through His love. Remember, just like you and I are raising our own imperfect children, God is also raising tons of imperfect children that includes all of humanity. We are the imperfect children of God but perfected and righteous only in His love.

Give thanks to Jesus Christ our Lord and Savior. Now, move on with your life with His love and support, and be confident. And if God asks you to do anything, obey Him for your own good. Obey Him for your blessings. His love for you will never change whether you obey Him or not. He loves you unconditionally. His forgiveness never changes, but your blessings on this earth is all depending on works of obedience. Listen to Him and obey His voice because all the blessing of God on this planet are dependent on your works of obedience.

> Now, Israel, what does the Lord your God require from you, but to fear the Lord your God, to walk in all His ways and love Him, and to serve the Lord your God with all your heart and with all your soul, and to keep the Lord's commandments and His statutes which I am commanding you today for your good?
>
> (Deuteronomy 10:12–13, NKJV)

> Walk in obedience to all that the Lord your God has commanded you, so that you may live and prosper and prolong your days in the land that you will possess.
>
> (Deuteronomy 5:33, NIV)

> But he who looks into the perfect law of liberty and continues in it and is not a forgetful hearer but a doer of the work, *this one will be blessed in what he does.*
>
> (James 1:25, NKJV)

Now, I pray to God without being ashamed of myself. I give all the praise to my savior Jesus. "Thank you, Lord."

As God is alive, His word is alive. And His "Word" will prove to you, He is alive.

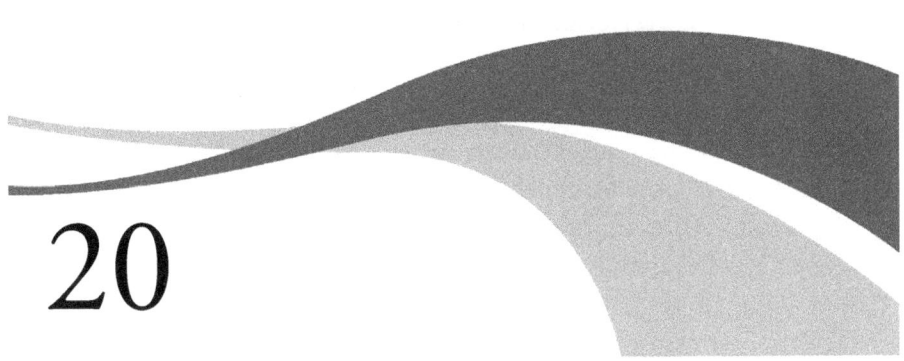

20

Court Case: Why Did You Come to Me?

In 2001, we purchased our home in a new development area. It was a beautiful new home that required us to put in a lawn, garden, fence, and many other items. I was looking for a contractor to do work for our house. One day, I stopped by one of our new neighbor's home. She was having a contractor installing a sprinkler system in her yard and he was also her neighbor.

He was a small businessman who builds semi-custom homes as his main source of income. He seemed friendly, kind, and appeared to be an honest person. I asked her how much she was paying for the sprinkler job. She said he is cheaper than the other contractors she met so far. Additionally, he is not charging her any of taxes because he can only work after his main work is done.

With that information, my husband and I decided to have a talk with him. We met with him and explained to him what kind of work we wanted him to do for us. We wanted him to put up a fence in our backyard, an indoor fireplace mantle, and a shelf above the fireplace for a television set.

The next day, he stopped by our house and measured everything. He then made his assessment and he charged us $1,200 for the fence, $250 for the fireplace mantle and a shelf. For the fireplace mantle, he wanted us to find a picture for him as a reference, so he would know what type of mantle he needed to make for us.

The total cost for all the work was $1450. I didn't mind this price at all. As a matter of fact, I kind of like it because his fees were about $200 less than others who gave us an estimate. We asked him for a contract, but he said we didn't need a contract. We did ask him a few more times for a contract, but he insisted to us that we wouldn't need one.

He ensured us that he would not do us any wrong. So, we stop asking him about a contract because we didn't want to offend him. We didn't want him to get an impression that we didn't trust him. Besides, we didn't think that he would do us any wrong because we were neighbors. So, we had verbal agreement.

Since he could only work during his spare time, we asked him how long it would take him to complete the work. He told us it will take him no more than two weeks to finish all the work. The next morning, he stopped by for a short while, dug a few holes for the fence post, and left for his main job. Again, he did the same thing the next morning.

On some days, he showed up in the evening and work for about half an hour and went home. Some days, he didn't even show up at all. Two weeks had passed and the fencing work wasn't even close to being finished.

We were not happy at all about his delays, but we didn't make an issue of it because he charged us less than other contractors, and we understood he only could come when he finished his main job for the day. We believed that he may have too much work from his main job, but we began to realize that we might have made a big mistake in hiring and trusting him.

The work really got delayed! But as long as he finished the work before my mother-in-law visited us, we decided not to make an issue of it. My mother-in-law was scheduled to visit us from another state the following month.

It took him little more than three weeks to finish just the fence. I should say it took him nearly a month. One evening, he stopped by our house and showed me an invoice. The total was nearly $1,900! It was divided as $1,200 for the fence, $250 for the mantle, and shelf, which was $1,450, and I do not remember the exact amount at this moment, but it was in between $400 to $450 of additional materials and taxes.

I was in shock! And I asked him why he charged us more than what we negotiated. He said he spent more money for fencing materials and for the taxes.

Then, at that very moment, he demanded me to pay him the full amount. I told him we would pay him when he finished all the work, and we cannot pay him more than what we negotiated. He got very angry and started to scream and yell at me to pay him the full $1,900 at that very moment.

I told him I couldn't pay him that very moment! But he kept insisting that I pay him in full that very second. He was proven to be a very bad man. Finally, I told him I needed to have a talk with my husband and asked for him to give me the invoice, but he didn't give it to me and he left.

That evening, my husband came home from a business trip. I shared with my husband what had happened. We talked, and we were looking for better way to solve the issue. We discussed to pay him $1,000 and, since he said he spent more money for the fence materials, we decided to raise him $250 more than what we initially negotiate. So, total came out to be $1,700. At this point, we didn't like what he was doing to us, but we didn't have any better choices. We wanted to settle this problem as peacefully as possible.

That same evening, my husband created a contract and went to his house. My husband told him if he signs the contract, we will give him a $1,000 check and will pay him $250 more than we had originally agreed. According to my husband, this guy was very angry because we asked him to sign the contract. He did sign it. My husband hand him a $1,000 check and an extra copy of contract to him, but he rejected the contract.

Now, we thought he was pretty happy with the extra $250 we were paying him. After a few days, he called and said he cannot build us a fireplace mantle and a shelf. He said the wood would cost him more than he expected. He said some wood cost more than others, and he cannot build a fireplace mantle like the picture we gave to him.

You see, it didn't make any sense to us because he told us to find a picture for the fireplace mantle and when we showed it to him in the beginning, he clearly said to us there would be no problem at all!

So, I asked him why he didn't mention it in the beginning. He didn't give me any answer. I asked him a few more questions about the wood and told him to use the cheapest wood as possible and make it as simple as possible. He said he would do that.

By this time, I didn't want to deal with him anymore. I just wanted him to finish the work, so we can move on with our life.

My mother-in-law was expected to be at our house within 2 weeks. We needed to have our house ready for our special guest. We asked him to finish his work as soon as possible. At this time, it had been little more than one month.

Honesty speaking, my husband and I were fed up with this guy. We realized that he was very dishonest. We felt that he didn't have any morals at all. He didn't feel any shame at all. I was wondering how in the world anyone could have thick skin as this man.

One evening, he brought over a few different pieces of woods for the mantle and acted like he was adjusting the pieces together. He then said he will be back with all the pieces. I thought he was finally going to finish his work, but we were in for yet another big surprise. The next day, he called and said he didn't think he could finish the work. "*What?*"

"*What does he want from us this time?*" He said he was afraid to build a TV shelf because he doesn't think that shelf would support the weight of the TV. I explained to him that it should not be a problem. He insisted he doesn't want to build the shelf because he doesn't want to be responsible for our TV. He said, if the TV dropped down, he may be the one who has to pay for the TV.

We knew this guy wasn't telling the truth. He is a housebuilder, and he knew when a builder makes a cutout in the wall for a TV above a fireplace; he has to build it to support the weight of a TV the size of the cutout. He knew this very well because his house has almost the same size cutout for a TV above his fireplace, just like ours.

He also knew we were running out of time before our guest arrived. He may have thought that we might offer him more money if he said he couldn't do it. At this point, we did not want to deal with him at all! But we did ask him to finish the work more than dozen times and told him to use the cheapest wood as possible, but we realized he would not do any more work until we offered him more money.

We told him if he didn't want to finish the work he didn't have to, but we also were not going to pay him remaining balance. He got very angry. He wanted to be paid all the remaining balance without finishing all the work (fireplace mantle and a shelf). He continually made phone calls for the payment several times, and he also wanted us to send him a copy of the contract, which my husband offered him before and he didn't want it.

We didn't have enough time to get a new contractor to finish the work before my mother-in-law visited us. When she visited us, we had the TV on the floor. She brought some video tape with her to show us our family from Florida, but we couldn't see any of her tapes because the TV and VCR were not set up for her.

After my mother-in-law visited us, we went to Home Depot to buy a premade fireplace mantle and some wood to make a shelf to finish the work. That's how simple it was. And the TV was placed above the fireplace for years without any problems.

Falling into the Trap of the Devil

The season had changed. With the Spring weather, people were outside to work on their gardens. I was working on my garden just like everyone else. One day, I met a new neighbor lady who moved into the house just next to ours. She started to tell me what she heard about us. She said, she heard that we didn't pay the guy who did all this work for us. I was shocked and couldn't believe what I was hearing.

He told many lies about us. When my husband came home that evening, I shared it with him. This was the beginning of my spiritual mistake. Over the next couple of days, I ran into more people and they were saying more things to me. Well, my biggest mistake was paying attention to what people were saying and worrying about what people might think of us. At this time, I was pretty upset at him.

Instead of keeping my mouth shut from what I heard each day, whenever my husband came home, I shared it with my husband. One day, I was walking to the mailbox, and I ran into this guy. I decided to confront him. I asked why he went around telling all those lies about us. He started to shout and made all kinds of false accusations about us. I was so upset all day, and again, that evening, I shared all to my husband, but while I was sharing, I heard this thundering voice in my spirit.

> "Tremble, and do not sin; meditate in your heart upon your bed, *and be still.*"
> (Psalm 4:4, NASB)

From that split moment, I knew something was wrong, but I let it go because I was too upset to pay any attention to the voice of God. God was warning me to keep my mouth shut and not share this with my husband. Even though God warned me to not share anything with my husband, I kept on sharing it with him and thought, *What could go wrong with this by sharing it with my husband? After all, he is my husband and has a right to know.*

What I didn't realize was, I was provoking my husband into anger until it was too late. And now this guy became our main subject to talk about every evening.

Instead of praying to God to seek His peace and wisdom, I spent all of my energy and time on this demonic stuff. Oh yes, I did pray, but I didn't pay any attention to my prayer. I allowed unhealthy thoughts to run through my mind all day and night and continually talked about him. Of course, the more we talked about him, the more we were getting upset at him. The more we were feeding each other with what the devil wanted to feed us, and we got angrier.

Now, ever since I started hearing about all the lies from my neighbors, I felt so uncomfortable to walk around our community. I felt like everyone was pointing their fingers at me. Worst of all, I felt so uncomfortable to go to the mailbox to check our own mail. I was a prisoner in my own community. This was upsetting me so much that I just wanted to defend myself, but I couldn't.

It seemed like everyone was believing him. It seemed like everyone was talking bad about me and my husband. I felt that we needed to do something about it to set things straight. Somehow, I felt I needed to stop him from spreading lies about us, resulting that we even started to talk about contacting a lawyer. Then,

"No weapon formed against you shall prosper,
And every tongue which rises against you in judgment You shall condemn."
(Isaiah 54:17, NKJV)

I clearly heard it. Deep in my spirit, I heard God speaking to me, but I ignored it again and decided to contact a lawyer. Close to three weeks had passed, but we still had not heard from the lawyer. So, we decided to contact our lawyer to find out what had happened. The lawyer's assistant told us they had not sent a letter because the lawyer went on vacation. The assistant told us she could send a letter if we wanted. We told her we would wait until the lawyer returned from vacation.

Later, we realized that God was providing more time for us to think wisely to cancel sending a letter, so we could avoid all the troubles and headaches that were waiting for us. But we didn't catch this until it was too late and fell into a trap the devil had set for us.

About a week later, after we contacted the lawyer office, my husband went to check the mail and there was a copy of a letter from our lawyer. The letter got sent to the contractor and a copy of the letter was sent to us. When my husband handed me a letter and said, "Here is the copy of the letter from our lawyer." When I held that letter in my hand, I knew what I felt. I felt such a horrible darkness come over me. I knew then something was totally and awfully wrong.

I opened it and started reading the letter. That letter itself didn't say much. It only said that he should not go around spreading lies about us and if he continued, we may have to take further action. But I know how this letter made me feel. It made me feel such horrible darkness. I didn't know what it was, but I knew for sure something was very wrong. I just felt it. Something went very and very wrong.

Lawsuit

And within a few days, we received a document from the small claims court! He sued us. When I received the court document, I instantly knew this was the darkness that I felt. He was suing us for $750 as an unpaid balance. We couldn't believe this! We were questioning how in the world he could sue us? After all, he didn't even finish the work. We were in shock!

I knew, I must pray to God to seek His wisdom. This does mean I didn't pray. Absolutely not! I did pray to God for the entire situation! From the beginning of the verbal agreement, but I was praying more out of habit than faith.

I asked God to help us to win our case, but at the same time, I prayed to God to give him a conviction for the wrong he did to us. I said to God, "Father, give him a conviction to change his mind to drop the lawsuit. Although he doesn't know you, he has a spirit created in your image and your likeness."

In "Matthew 6:45, you say, You cause the sun to rise on the evil and the good and sends rain on the righteous and the unrighteous. Just as you give rain and sun to this evil guy, I know you also can speak to him through a dream or something. So, Father, can you speak to his conscience?" I asked God to convict him to drop the case.

Missing God's Answers

Every time when I prayed for the court situation, God started to remind me about one particular sister we knew from church. She was the church head door greeter coordinator. I could not figure out why God was showing me this lady every time when I prayed for our court case. I shared it with my husband a couple of times, but he didn't have any clue either why God was showing me this lady. Since I could not figure it out, I totally let it go out of my mind.

I prayed a few more days, and this time, God gave me an idea. His idea was to ask this same sister for a letter. To give us a written letter about the contractor who kept changing the agreement. You see, she was not a witness at the beginning of our verbal contract, but she was the witness from the first time when he changed his agreement with us. She knew from that moment. Each time he changed his agreement, the following Sunday we went to church and shared it with her to pray for us.

I shared it with my husband to ask for a letter from this sister. He didn't think we need a letter from her. First, he did not want to bother her, and he believed, as long as we have a contract, we would win the case. With that answer from my husband, once again, I let it go out of my mind completely.

By this time, God probably was shaking His head with empathy. God probably was saying He couldn't believe what He was witnessing. I was dull as solid rock. I just didn't get it. God kept trying to reach me to help, but I was not paying any attention to Him at all.

Surprisingly, a few days later, this very sister called me! She never called me before. If she needed to communicate to us about door greeter coordination, she always contacted my husband. She never called me! But I received a phone call from her!

She asked me what she can do to help me. I was in shock! And asked her, "Why are you asking if I need any help from you?" She said, "Every morning, when I prayed for you, God told me that you are in some kind of trouble and you need my help."

I was so happy and excited to hear from her about this. I explained to her about our court case, and as we talked, she recalled all the incidents. We talked for a while and she suggested that she should pray for the court case. After that, we ended our conversation and hung up the phone. "Oh, my goodness," God provided me one more opportunity to ask for a letter, but I completely let it go.

Well, finally, the court day had arrived and just as you may have guessed it, we lost the case. It blew up in our face. Somehow, the judge didn't give us any chance to defend ourselves. The judge already made her decision before we even attempted to defend ourselves. Each and every time we wanted to talk, the judge shut us down. Even with the contract paper, it didn't help us out at all!

We just couldn't believe what was happing to us. The contract didn't guarantee anything to us at all. Later, I realized if anyone depended on man's judgments and systems, it will fail us. Man's judgment cannot be perfect as God's. Man and his system are imperfect because men's judgment can be totally wrong and biased.

Blaming God

When we came home, I went straight to my bedroom to pour out my heart to God. I was not going to just cry out, but I was determined to find out what went wrong. I knew, I was right as far as the contract goes. We didn't do anything wrong. I sat on the floor before God and asked Him why in the world this was happening to us.

I cry out in an extremely loud voice and I pounded the floor, "Pound and pound" and "Cry and cry", and spoke to God in a loud voice, "You know the truth, God. When we made the contract, you've heard everything. You heard what he said to us and what we said to him."

> I quoted to God, "He who planted the ear, does He not hear? He who formed the eye, does He not see."
>
> (Psalm 94:9, NASB)

"Didn't you say this? If your word is true and you heard and saw everything, why in the world didn't you help us to win this case? Didn't you hear what this guy promised to us? I know you heard everything. You heard what he said and what we said. You are not fair. You should have done something to help me. You know, morally and legally, we didn't do anything wrong. We shouldn't have lost this case. We should have won the case. I don't understand why you did not do anything to help us."

I cried, cried, and cried. God allowed me to pour my heart to Him. He allowed me to say whatever I needed to say to Him and how I wanted to say to Him.

Some time had passed, and slowly, quietness settled in my heart. And then, God began to ask me some questions with an extremely gentle voice. The first question He asked me was, "Why did you come to me? Why did you come to me to pray?"

"???"

"Did you come to see my face? Did you come to touch my hand? Did you come to me for the instruction?" Or did you come to me, so I can do everything for you?"

"???"

Then He said, "I did try to help you."

"How did you try to help me?" I asked.

He told me, "I try to help you three different times. I try to grab your attention with this particular sister three times. Two times with you and one with her." Right then, I immediately realized who He was talking about. He was talking about that very sister. Then I told God, "Though I missed your help, you should still have done something for me. You should still have helped me!"

He told me, "If I would have helped you, you wouldn't learn the lesson."

I told God, "That's not true! I would still learn. You should help me out first, but you didn't. You said nothing is impossible for you and I believed you. If I have all the powers like you have, I would have done it different than what you did." Then He asked me how I would have done it. I told God, "If one of my sons is in the similar situation, I would have rescued him first and then corrected him later."

Then God laid out a scenario for me with a question. He said, "Let's say, one of your sons is having a problem with a boy at school and he asked for your help. You advised him to stay away from the harasser and to stay out of trouble. He listens to you for a while, but one day, your son decides to confront the boy and it caused him to receive a huge black eye. When he comes home and rings the door bell, 'ding dong', you open the door for him and see a huge black eye on his face.

"Who would be more hurting? Him? The one who has a black eye on his face? Or you, who is looking at your son's black eye? Do you feel more hurt than your son? Do you?"

At that very moment, I realized how much I hurt the Father. Tears were running down my face. He went on to say, "Your son may be hurt physically, but are you not hurt more emotionally?"

"Yes, Father, yes, I would be hurt more deeply. It would have hurt me more."

Then He told me, "I was hurt too. It was very painful for me to watch you. I have all the power to rescue you, but I had to watch you painfully while the devil was beating you. I had to stay out of it for you to learn a lesson. I had to stay out of it, so you would learn how important it is to listen to my instruction."

He said, "I know I have all the power and abilities to do anything for my children, but I am limited to get involved with my children's life because they do not follow my instruction.

"They pray and ask for my help but most of them do not listen to my direction. They expect me to do everything for them." He said, "When my children pray, I give them instruction. I give them directions. And if they follow my instruction and direction, they will receive a miracle."

Then He said, "Go restudy the Words! How miracles occurred in the Bible. All the miracles occurred in the Bible because they listened to my instruction and followed!"

His Specific Instruction to His People

"How did Moses divided the water? Did I not give him specific instruction? Did I not give him instruction to raise his staff over the Red Sea? (Exodus 14:16). When he did, I divided the water (Exodus 14:21). Did I not give Aaron specific instruction? Didn't I tell him to throw his staff down before Pharaoh, so it turned into a serpent? (Exodus 7:9). Aaron listened to my instruction and did exactly what I spoke, and then the miracles happened!"

> Then the Lord spoke to Moses, "Say to *Aaron*, 'Stretch out your hand with your rod over the streams, over the rivers, and over the ponds, and cause frogs to come up on the land of Egypt.'" So *Aaron stretched* out his hand over the waters of Egypt, and the frogs came up and covered the land of Egypt.
> (Exodus 8:5, NKJV)

Aaron, not Moses, needed to stretch out His hand with the rod and then miracles happened. And also, without stretching out his hand, no miracles happened, so Aaron needed to stretch his hand over the waters of Egypt, then there were miracles.

More example God led me to:

> So the Lord said to Moses and Aaron, "Take for yourselves handfuls of ashes from a furnace and let *Moses* scatter it toward the heavens in the sight of Pharaoh. And it will become fine dust in all the land of Egypt, and it will cause boils that break out in sores on man and beast throughout all the land of Egypt." Then they took ashes from the furnace and stood before Pharaoh, and *Moses scattered* them toward heaven. And they caused boils that break out in sores on man and beast.

> And the magicians could not stand before Moses because of the boils, for the boils were on the magicians and on all the Egyptians.
> (Exodus 9:8, NKJV)

God gave specific instructions. This time, God wanted Moses, not Aaron, to scatter ashes toward the heavens, not to the ground. And then, when Moses scattered ashes toward heaven, the miracle happened.

He led me to a story about David. When David inquired of the Lord, God gave him specific instruction on how to defeat the Philistine.

> Therefore David inquired of the Lord, and He said, "You shall not go up; circle around behind them and come upon them in front of the mulberry trees. And it shall be, when you hear the sound of marching in the tops of the mulberry trees, then you shall advance quickly. For then the Lord will go out before you to strike the camp of the Philistines." *And David did so, as the Lord commanded him*; and he drove back the Philistines from Geba as far as Gezer.
> (2 Samuel 5:23–25, NKJV)

When David did as God gave him instruction, God defeated his enemies. How about Joshua? (Joshua 6) God also gave Joshua specific instruction on how to overtake Jericho. Joshua did exactly as God told him to do and received miracles.

Miracles Will Occur Only If

Then God said to me, "Many of my children do understand about miracles and they do want the miracles for their lives, but they totally miss the most important fact about miracles. They miss the very important point on how miracles occurred. *All the miracles occurred because they believed me and followed my instructions!* My children want the miracles, but they do not follow my instructions. They want the miracles, but miracles will not occur unless otherwise they pay attention to what I am saying and follow what I tell them."

He pointed out James 2:20. "Faith without work is dead faith," which means, "Faith without obedience, no miracles." Again, I was shocked! Somehow, I wanted and expected God to do miracles for me without listening to His instruction. I was expecting a miracle without following His direction.

I realized where I missed God. I didn't listen to His answer. I didn't pay attention to His instruction. I expected Him to do everything for me without following His direction.

God continued, "You prayed to me to convict this guy either through dreams or something to drop the lawsuit. I did answer you! But what makes you think he will listen to me when he is not my own, but you, as my own child, don't even listen to me?"

At this point, I was crying deeply in sorrow not because I lose my court case but because how I hurt my God. Consequences of my mistakes hurt Him more than it hurt me. I felt His love all over the room. His love overwhelmed me so deeply. My tears ran down on my cheeks like thick liquid. That thick liquid tears were mixed with His love, compassion, kindness, and all His goodness, I couldn't describe it with any words.

I didn't realize, just as we get hurt when our children get hurt, how we hurt God when we get hurt. At this point, I couldn't argue with Him about His justice and love. I could only ask God for forgiveness for not listening to His answer.

God's love and peace were filling my heart. I wasn't angry at this guy anymore, nor at me, or at my husband, nor at that judge. God's understanding of the entire situation was so comforting. I was comforted completely because God heard, saw, and knew everything between this guy and us. God knew what was true and what was a lie. God knew who was truthful of this whole situation. That meant so much to me, and it was truly comforting to me.

I went downstairs to share it with my husband. When he heard how God was hurt because of us, tears were running down his cheeks. He started to cry deeply without crying a sound.

After that, I needed to bring one thing to closure to my children. At this time, our children were thirteen and twelve years of age. They knew about the court case, and they were praying for it also. We assured them we would win because we did not do anything wrong, and in addition to that, God would help us to win because God is our Father. But when they learned that we lost the case, they didn't know what to say to us.

My biggest concern was I didn't want my children to question about God's existence and His abilities. That was my biggest fear. After I had short conversation with my husband, I immediately took time to explain it to them.

I explained to them we lost the case not because God didn't help us. We lost our case because we didn't listen to God's instruction and direction. I told them, I learned a very valuable lesson of how important it is to listen to God when we pray. They clearly understood what had happened.

That evening, when we all got ready to go to bed, I asked our oldest son to pray for me. Pray for me to have the biggest spiritual ear to hear God better. I told him, "I don't want to miss out on God's instructions anymore. The consequence of not listening to God was very painful." Then he said to me, "Sure, Mom, I will pray for you, but what size ears do you want? Four feet?" With his smart remark, we all laughed.

This very important spiritual lesson that I learned from this incident is how important it is to listen to God. It is not about how much we pray, how we pray, where we pray, when we pray, or who prays for us or with us. Prayer is all about, "Are we paying attention to what God is saying?"

Many people make mistakes like I did. They are missing out from God's answers because they fail to listen to God. They are missing out because they, somehow, expect God to do everything for them instead of listening to His instructions.

God is eager to help you more than you expect from him. You must remember to pay attention to His answers and follow His instructions. Then, you'll see many miracles in your life. He promises.

> Call to Me, and *I will answer you*, and show you great and mighty things, which you do not know.
> (Jeremiah 33:3, NKJV)

> Why do you call me, "Lord, Lord," and do not do what I say?
> (Luke 6:46, NIV)

> He replied, "Blessed rather are those who hear the word of God and obey it."
> (Luke 11:28, NIV)

> Then Jesus said, "Whoever has ears to hear, let them hear."
> (Mark 4:9, NIV)

Just remember, all the miracles occurred in the Bible because our spiritual forefathers listened to God and did exactly as He had said. Listen to His answer and do as He say, you'll see so many mighty miracles happening to your life.

> *As God is alive, His word is alive. And His "Word" will prove to you, He is alive.*

21

Jericho March

One day, I received a call from a fellow sister I knew from a local church. She wanted me to meet her at a new housing site that was being developed in our area. I drove to this site to meet her. She took me into one of the brand-new homes that happened to be unlocked. Perhaps, one of real estate agents forgot to lock the house. We went inside the house and then she explained why she invited me to that particular house.

She said because they really wanted that house, that her husband and her had come to that house before, and did a Jericho March around that house. She said the seller was asking nearly $500,000, but they could only afford to pay up $360,000, so they decided to do march around that house and claim it for $360,000.

She further explained what she wanted me to do for her. She wanted me to pray for her and do the Jericho March with her. I was in shock and was lost for words at that moment. When I was ready to speak, I asked her this. "Okay, can you answer these questions for me? If you can answer my questions, then I will do the Jericho March with you. What if you are the one who is selling this house? Would you sell it for that reduced price?" She didn't answer my question.

"Let's say, you have the obligation to take care of your family and to pay the wages to all the workers who built this house. Would you sell this house for that price?" She didn't say anything and finally she understood the point I was driving. We walked out of that house and I prayed for her to find a good house, which she could afford to buy and then we left that place.

I often hear about people who would do a Jericho March, so they could get someone's property at a very unreasonable price. These folks, while well intended, have a huge misunderstanding of the meaning of the Jericho March. They think the walls of Jericho fell because Joshua and the Israelites did the march around the city wall. But this thinking is only partially true.

The most important truth is that the marching around the city of Jericho was the will of God. It came down because it was God's will for it to come down.

> You shall march around the city, all you men of war; you shall go all around the city once. This you shall do six days. And seven priests shall bear seven trumpets of rams' horns before the ark. But the seventh day you shall march around the city seven times, and the priests shall blow the trumpets. It shall come to pass, when they make a long blast with the ram's horn, and when you hear the sound of the trumpet, that all the people shall shout with a great shout; then the wall of the city will fall down flat. And the people shall go up every man straight before him.
> (Joshua 6:3–5, NKJV)

God revealed His plan to Joshua on what to do and how to do it, and as they obeyed God's plan, the walls of Jericho came crashing to the ground. Its wall collapsed because it was God's plan! God made the plan to hand over the city of Jericho to the Israelites—its king and its fighting men and everything in it.

It didn't come down because people marched around the city wall! No! God gave them the command, and their faith in the words of God, and their obedience to God caused Jericho walls to tumble down. This is how this happened.

We need to be careful how we apply God's word into our situation(s). Just because the Word was written in the Bible doesn't mean we just claim to get something for nothing. By mealy saying, "I believe the Word, and I am going to march around it to get a house for an unreasonable price."

If that's how we acquire things from God, why don't we march around the Empire State building, so we can buy it at an unreasonable price? Why don't we march around it and possess it for free?

If that is how the word of God works, then we should say, "I believe the word of God, so I am going to walk on water just like Peter!" (Matthew 14:27–29). We should walk on water to surprise and convince all nonbelievers of the gospel. Why not? Then everyone would believe in Jesus.

Why don't we do that? We don't do that because we know we can't walk on water just because we say, "Peter walked on water, and I believe I can too!" You know, you can't walk on water just because it is written in the Bible and you proclaim it.

Let's think about this for a moment. What is the difference the between marching around the city of Jericho and walking on the water? If anyone has faith to march around someone's property to buy it at an unbelievable price, *then with that same faith*, one should walk on water to surprise everyone around them! We should all do that.

You see, faith doesn't work like that, but many Christians proclaim they will do a Jericho march on someone's property to receive a miracle from God, but no one claims they will walk on water to display God's glory for world to see!

You see, doing the Jericho march might seem like one has great faith because it doesn't reveal the results of one's faith immediately, but walking on the water, everyone can see one's true faith immediately. The minute one places his foot in the water, it instantly reveals one's true faith. This is the very reason why many don't proclaim they can walk on the water to prove their faith. But it is much easier to proclaim they have a great faith to do a Jericho march.

Let's examine something here, both miracles, marching around the city of Jericho and walking on water, had fundamental special elements. These elements were, first, God "spoke" it. Both miracles happened because God spoke it to initiated, and the men believed the word and acted on it.

But if you want to acquire someone's property by just marching around it, it will not work unless God "speaks" to initiate it. If God didn't speak it to you, it will require more than to march around it to acquire it. It requires God's wisdom to negotiate the price and terms to acquire it at a favorable price.

You may want to say, "It is written, and I believe it." Yes, it is written, but it still must be initiated by God. It needs to be inspired by the Spirit of God to your heart. God must tell you to do it even though it is written in the Bible. If God tells you to march around like Joshua, and you believe it, and act on His Word, then it will work. It will work because God purposed it to work, not because you claim the written word to work.

I'll share with you one true story. I knew a brother in Christ. He was a single man very close to forty years old at the time. He had been looking for a spouse for quite a while. One day, my husband and I along with this single brother went out to lunch with one of the pastors we knew. As we were having lunch, this brother told our pastor friend, that in Jesus's name, he claimed one sister from our church to be his wife.

The pastor told this man, "You cannot claim her or any women to be your wife in Jesus's name. This will not work. While you may desire this woman to be your spouse, she may have another man in mind that she wants to marry." He then explained that God has given each of us a free will to choose and that He will not violate this.

Some believe, like this brother, that as long as they say, "I believe," they think they have great faith. They don't even realize they have a wrong faith. Their faith does not line up with the word of God, will of God, and character of God; therefore, it will not work! They are only enticed by their own greed.

> "But each one is tempted when he is drawn away
> by his own desires and enticed"
> (James 1:14, NKJV)

And then when their greedy desire, (false faith), does not work, they get angry at God. Their foolish faith has become a stumbling block for them.

> "The foolishness of a man twists his way, and his
> heart frets against the LORD."
> (Proverbs 19:3, NKJV)

You see, faith doesn't work like that! If you believe for a healing, you just simply "believe the word" and receive your healing. It will work because healing has already been purchased on the cross. It only involves your faith in the word of God to receive it.

But if you believe to buy one's property for an unreasonable price, then all three must come into agreement—God, the other person, and you. And when God has a special purpose for His kingdom, God will initiate for all three to agree in order for it to work. Otherwise, without the agreement from all three, it will not work.

God is not going to take advantage of other people to give what you want just because you did a Jericho march. He is not going to force His will on other people to make things happen for you.

Remember, God is a God of love! Just as He considers your situation, this God of love also considers another person's situation. This is the very reason why some people's faith doesn't work because they are operating in greed and not in love.

> "For in Christ Jesus neither circumcision nor
> uncircumcision avails anything, but faith working through love."
> (Galatians 5:6, NKJV)

And some believers think, just because they are a child of God, they are more special than nonbelievers. They think they can receive special favors from God in any situation and in any way. This is the reason why some do a Jericho march without hearing from God. Sure, His children are His favorite, but it doesn't mean that God will allow His children to take advantage of others. Remember, God is a God of love towards all people.

> Never take advantage of poor and destitute laborers, whether they are fellow Israelites or foreigners living in your towns.
> (Deuteronomy 24:14, NLT)

> But love your enemies, do good, and lend, hoping for nothing in return; and your reward will be great, and you will be sons of the Most High. For He is kind to the unthankful and evil.
> (Luke 6:35, NKJV)

> For He makes His sun rise on the evil and on the good and sends rain on the just and on the unjust.
> (Matthew 5:45b, NKJV)

God asks each of us to be salt and light in our world. Don't forget, God has great concern for others just as He has great concern for you. Don't make the mistake or misunderstand God's blessing. Just because God is your Heavenly Father, it doesn't mean God will give you anything you ask without love.

God is a God of love, and He has great love for all people. We too must have great love for all people. We should not take advantage of lost souls. We must not think because we have God's favor, God will give to us anything that violates His love for others.

> "Jesus answered and said to them, 'You are mistaken, not knowing the Scriptures nor the power of God'."
> (Matthew 22:29, NKJV)

Let's understand the Word and His power in the correct way. His Word and power will work for His children only when you apply "love" into your faith. And when you apply His love to your faith, then you'll receive anything you ask in His name.

> "For in Christ Jesus neither circumcision nor uncircumcision avails anything, but faith working through love."
>
> (Galatians 5:6, NKJV)

In conclusion, I like to ask you one question? Would you want someone to do Jericho walk on your property in order to get it for free from you? Would you? Ask God with love.

As God is alive, His word is alive. And His "Word" will prove to you, He is alive.

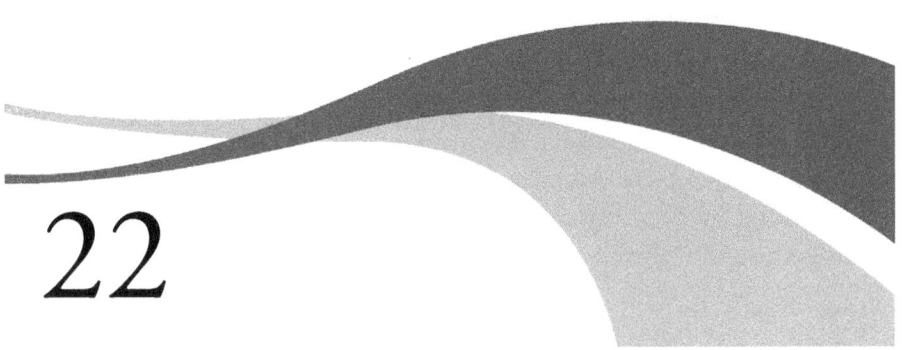

22

I No Longer Wish to Teach Her: God's Justice

When we moved into our new community, I met a lady who was a nonbeliever. (I'll refer to her as Lee). Lee's entire family attended church with her being the only exception. She never attended church because she held very negative views toward church and was critical and judgmental.

I decided to pray for her salvation. In addition to prayers, whenever I had an opportunity to talk with her, I shared my personal testimony as a way to witness Jesus Christ to her. As I shared, she listened to me with much interest.

In seven years of praying, the Lord provided me an opportunity to lead her to repeat the sinner's prayer. She accepted Jesus as her Lord and Savior.

She started attending the church that one of her sisters attended. Three months after she received Christ, she stopped by my house to ask me to teach her the Bible. I agreed to do it because over time, I'd learned that she had the tendency to open herself up to different spiritual things. She often talked about dreams and tried to predict the dream. If something happened to her, she tried to connect it to her dreams.

Knowing this, I felt that I really needed to teach her the truth. So, I agreed to teach her. At this time, I was volunteering at my church as the Asian/America minister, and every Tuesday, I volunteered and invested my time at a retreat center. We agreed to meet at the retreat center every Tuesday to study the Bible.

Knowing she has tendency to open herself to different spiritual things, I taught her the importance of the Word of God and emphasize the need to believe the Word. I wanted to make sure her faith got grounded not on visions, or dreams, or any other thing, but on the Word of God.

I also taught her, more than anyone I ever taught before, on the subject of false prophets, false miracles, and false dreams in order to prevent her from falling into any false teaching.

As time went by, I learned she not only attended my Bible study, but also many other Bible studies throughout the week. I didn't mind it because I thought she was hungry for God's Word.

Then I learned, in addition to all kinds of other Bible studies, she also attended a prayer group which was practicing a weird form of spirituality. At this time, I kind of knew something was wrong about this group, but I wasn't quite sure what was wrong. I told her not to participate in this group, but she attended anyways.

She believed in herself that she was able to tell what was true or false. She said to me, "You don't have to worry about it. I know what to pick, and I know what to eat what not to eat" (meaning she had the ability to discern true or false).

As our Bible study continued, I began to clearly notice she didn't come to Bible study to learn, rather she came to steal Bible knowledge to use it to brag about her spirituality. (Later, I told this to her face). Her reason was she noticed other's reaction of her Bible knowledge and this provided her a sense of pride.

When she went to other Bible studies and shared what she learned from me, she saw their reaction of amazement. She liked their reaction. People, who were amazed at her knowledge, served Jesus for many years, but as she shared, she noticed they didn't know what she knew. This caused her to be very aggressive toward my Bible knowledge.

Now, I'm not saying I knew more than other teachers, but what I am saying is, what she shared was not known by the people in that group.

Besides her bad intentions of stealing, she often said, "God put you in my life to learn from you as quickly as possible and as much as possible. God must have a special purpose for me. I should have received Christ a long time ago. I wasted too much time. I believe God put you in my life to teach me all that you learned.

It took you almost twenty years to learn, but I could learn it from you in a very short time. I don't have to take a long time like you did. I believe, God put you in my life to teach me the scriptures, and God put another sister to teach me spirituality." She meant another lady who practiced the occult.

"God must have special plans for me." Somehow, she thought that she had a calling from God, but no one told her this, she just thought this in her own mind.

I'll share with you what I had discovered. People who attended this meeting, once or twice, came and told me what they were doing. As people walked into this house for prayer meeting, everyone needed to grab a small trash can and a box of tissue.

Then they sat down on the floor and began to force themselves to vomit in the trash can. Meaning they are vomiting up demons and sins. Some laid on the floor and shook their bodies violently to disfigure their body and made weird sounds very loudly to claim access to a spiritual realm.

Then when the leader lady laid her hands on a person, he or she needed to drop to the floor, shake violently, and start making weird sounds. Failure to do this had the others to believe he or she did not have any faith at all.

After I learned about all her bad intentions and this group, I was deeply bothered to sit with her for Bible study. I completely lost the desires to teach her because I had a deep concern. The concern I had was, since I knew what was wrong with this group, I did not want to equip her with good Bible knowledge that she would use for the occult.

Many times, I told her she shouldn't attend those meetings, but she looked at me as though I didn't know what I was talking about. She truly believed this group was a Bible-based group. Therefore, she continually attended this group meetings and was determined to learn their spiritual practices.

So, whenever she showed up for Bible class I was conducting, I tried not to give her the secret revelation God had given me. (Unfortunately, now she's involved deeply in this group).

In addition to all these concerns, I definitely noticed she took advantaged of my kindness. She took an excessive amount of my time, my resources, my knowledge, prayers, and energy, and she took them for granted. I never once received a "thank you" from her or she never reciprocated in anyway, even in a small way.

She acted like she deserved this from me and that I owed her this service. When she showed up for Bible study, she acted like she is doing me a favor by showing up. She stayed as long as three to four hours in order to take as much Bible revelation as she could consume. She called me at any time, she felt like it, even late at night to ask certain questions.

Sometimes, when I couldn't, or she couldn't be at the retreat center because of another obligation, she'd asked me to accommodate her schedule on a different day to teach her at my house. I did that to be kind and tried to be a good Christian, especially because she was a new believer.

I Decided to Pray to God

After five months of teaching her, I reached the point I could not handle this burden and anguish anymore. I prayed to God to release me from this unhealthy relationship. I could have stopped the Bible study without praying to God, but because I knew how important one soul is to His kingdom, and I didn't want to make this important decision without His approval.

I decided to take it to God. I said, "Father, I no longer have a desire to teach her. Please release me from this relationship. If she learns your Word only from me, I will continue. But as you know, Father, she goes all over the place to learn about the Bible. She is not only depending on me to feed her, she gets fed by many others. God, release me from this relationship."

I also prayed, "Father, when a farmer goes out and plant seed, he expects to receive a harvest. I planted much seed in her, but I know I won't receive any harvest from her. You know what she is doing. She's taking advantage of me.

"Father, even nonbelievers know how to treat others who help them. But not a single time did she offer me a cup of coffee, not even a tiny reciprocation. Instead, she acted as though she was doing me a favor by showing up for Bible study.

"Father, I poured my heart into this, my time, resources, knowledge, prayers, and energy. Where is my harvest? She is using me for her glorification and gain. Father, release me from this relationship. I no longer want to teach her. Release me from this unhealthy relationship." I prayed very honestly to God.

I knew that just because I helped someone doesn't mean my harvest will come from that person. His harvest—God's harvest—comes from all people, all directions, and all different methods. God knew my heart, I didn't teach her to receive anything, or for my honor, or exultation. I was just happy to teach her the word of God with an innocent and pure heart. Because I wanted her faith to be grounded in His Word, I eagerly taught her His truth.

One day as usual, I prayed to God to release me from this relationship. Then God answered, "Continue on teaching."

"What? Father, what did you not understand?" I went on and said, "Father, when a farmer goes out and plant seed, he expects to receive a harvest! Your word even says that a worker deserves his wages."

> What soldier has to pay his own expenses? What farmer plants a vineyard and doesn't have the right to eat some of its fruit? What shepherd cares for a flock of sheep and isn't allowed to drink some of the milk?
>
> (1 Corinthians 9:7, NLT)

> For the Scripture says, "You must not muzzle an ox to keep it from eating as it treads out the grain." And in another place, "Those who work deserve their pay!"
>
> (1 Timothy 5:18, NLT)

"You know, I won't receive anything from her. I know your harvest comes in all different forms and fashions, but I no longer want to teach her. I don't want to be used by her for bad intentions. Father, you know, she takes advantages of my kindness. She takes my kindness for granted. If she only depended on me to feed her a spiritual meal, I'd continue, but now she is being fed by many other people. Please release me from this relationship."

Then God went on and said, "Continue on teaching."

"Why, God? Why? I no longer want to do it." Now, I did sound like I was complaining.

Then God said, "I'll give you what you want through her."

"You'll give me what I want through her?"

"Yes, through her." (At this time, I was praying to God to open a new ministry for me, read Jehovah Jireh).

"How can you do that? How can you give me what I want through her?" "You know she is not that generous. You know she is not a giver." I spoke to Him very honestly.

This is her testimony. She said whenever she conducts any kind of business transaction with others, she must receive more than the other person. She must have, not equal, but at least one more than another person. If others make a better deal than her, it really bothers her.

She also said when she seizes an opportunity to gain something, she tries to get as much as she can. Hearing this from her and knowing her from my personal relationship, I wanted to know how God would be able to give me what I wanted through her!

"How can you give me what I want through her? How?" "I'll give to you through the people she knows."

"Though the people she knows?"

"Yes, through the people she knows. So, don't complain about how she goes to many different places for Bible study. What she's doing is actually preparing the way for your new ministry."

"Preparing for my new ministry?"

"Yes, when she goes to other Bible studies and talks about you, she is making you known unto people you don't know. Without knowing it, she is preparing those people to support your new ministry."

When I heard this from God, I no longer asked God to release me from that relationship. I shut my mouth and continually held my Bible study with much caution.

A little more than a month after I heard from God, I planned to travel to China for a missionary trip in mid-April. I told her that I couldn't hold our Bible study starting from the beginning of April. She wanted me to continue teaching until the week I was supposed to leave.

"When do you leave?"

"I leave in the middle of April."

"You still have time to teach me two more Tuesdays."

"No, not really. I need to prepare myself and buy gifts for my family." I planned to visit my family in South Korea before I go to China.

"It should not take you that much time for shopping. You can still hold Bible studies, right?"

I told her, "I may be able to, but I won't. I needed to take care of things before I go." Then she wanted to know what I planned to do about Bible study after I come back from China. I told her I really didn't know what I will do, and that I would give her a call if I resume it.

After I came back from China, I didn't contact her for a little more than a month, then she called and stopped by my house to make a suggestion. She said a few ladies whom she knew wanted to learn about the Bible from me. So, I told her I will no longer volunteer to do it, but if they willing to compensate me, then I would do it.

I said this to her, not because I needed the money, nor wanted the money, but I no longer wanted her to take advantage of me. I told her I will charge them $50 per person for a month. They all agreed.

We met every Tuesday for the Bible study. From this Bible study, I met some of the ladies who eventually supported my first independent ministry.

About a month and half into the Bible study, she came to ask me to go with her to pray for her friend JJ and this is how I met JJ (Read Jehovah Jira). One by one, God brought the things we needed to the new church. Through her friend JJ, God provided a worship sanctuary without a contract and rent free and a small podium. I am still using this podium.

Through her and her sister, God provided $600 to buy the first set of twenty chairs, three 72 × 29 inches tables, and a coffee pot. Through her, a pastor's wife, who heard about God opening of our new ministry, donated a refrigerator to the church. We replaced the refrigerator because it broke.

Through her, a lady who attended Bible class donated a couch set. We still use this. Through her, many more small donations came.

Close to one month of preparing for the new sanctuary, she came to see me. We had small talk, then she said, "Hey, that cross you put on the wall, don't you think it is too small?"

I said, "Yes, it is too small for that wall, but what choice do I have this time?" Then she went on said, "Hey, I just received the cross as a gift. I can donate it. I'll bring it to your house." Through her, God provided a cross to hang up on the wall. We still have this cross on the wall.

Wow! God knows how to compensate His children. It happened as God told me. "I will give you what you want through her." It was done as He said! God is the God of love, but God is also a God of justice! I also found it amusing that she prided herself on always getting the best in any deal, but God made sure I got the best part.

Don't Take Advantage of Other's Kindness

Some Christians make a similar mistake just like her. They take advantage of other Christian's goodness and kindness. Some portray themselves as needy and poor and use Jesus's teachings to take advantages of other believers. They take advantage of others by saying, "God will repay you for your kindness." Sure, God knows how to repay for one's kindness, but one should never use God's teaching to take advantage of others and refuse to do what is right. This is very wrong and even demonic.

Some received much help from believers and even from nonbelievers, but never reciprocate. Even nonbelievers know that taking advantages of others is wrong, but believers behave worse than the nonbelievers. Some believers take advantage of nonbelievers and say, "God bless me because I'm a believer." This is also wrong because God doesn't bless His children by taking advantages of others.

Let's look at what God says in this.

> All slaves should show full respect for their masters, so they will not bring shame on the name of God and his teaching. If the masters are believers, that is no excuse for being disrespectful. Those slaves should work all the harder because their efforts are helping other believers who are well loved.
> (1 Timothy 6:1–2, NLT)

If you work for a fellow Christian, there is no excuse to not do what is right. Fellow Christians doesn't mean, you'll be disrespectful and take advantage of a brother or sisters in Christ. As you just read the above scripture, you must do more to help fellow believers.

> Show your fear of God by *not taking advantage* of each other. I am the Lord your God.
> (Leviticus 25:17, NLT)

> And that in this matter *no one should wrong or take advantage of a brother or sister.* The Lord will punish all those who commit such sins, as we told you and warned you before.
> (1 Thessalonians 4:6, NIV)

> *Never take advantage* of poor and destitute laborers, whether they are fellow *Israelites or foreigners* living in your towns.
> (Deuteronomy 24:14, NLT)

Again, it doesn't matter what they are, who they are, we are taught to not take advantage of others, believers and nonbelievers. We must not take advantages of others to bring shame on His name and His teachings. God also said we should not foolishly allow anyone to take advantage of our kindness. The same applies to us. We must not take advantage of other's kindness.

We are taught to do what is right and be kind to others all the time. Do what is right and fair. If you know what is right but don't do it, it is a sin. Don't forget, God is a God of love, but God is also a God of justice too!

> "So it is a sin for the person who knows to do what is good (right) and doesn't do it"
> (James 4:17, HCSB)

How about you? Has someone taken advantage of you, but you can't avoid it because of your circumstances? Or someone took advantage of you and caused you lots of pain and loss of finances? And you don't know what to do? Whatever it is, take it to God. Let God know what you are going through or have gone through.

God knows how to bring justice to your situation. Just tell God, like I did. He knows what happened or is happening to you. He just wants you to come and lay it all out for Him. Let God be your judge. Let God display His justice on your situation.

> And will not God bring about justice for his chosen ones, who cry out to him day and night? Will he keep putting them off?
>
> (Luke 18:7, NIV)

> Yet the Lord longs to be gracious to you; therefore, he will rise up to show you compassion. For the Lord is a God of justice. Blessed are all who wait for him!
>
> (Isaiah 30:18, NIV)

God will arise for your justice. Just tell God. He will bring justice for you. We can see this from Jacob life on how God displayed His mighty justice on Jacob. You know that Jacob ran from his brother Esau after stealing his birthright blessing and was living with his uncle Laban. He lived there and worked for Laban for twenty years, while Laban took advantage of Jacob by changing his wages ten times!

> "For twenty years, I have worked in your household—fourteen years for your two daughters and six years for your flocks—and you have changed my wages ten times!"
>
> (Genesis 31:41, HCSB)

Genesis. 30:30 explains Laban had very little flocks before Jacob got there. When Jacob began to take care of Laban's flocks, his flocks increased tremendously under Jacob's care, but Jacob was treated very dishonestly. Can you imagine how Jacob felt? He was mistreated, humiliated, betrayed by his own uncle. In addition, he was put into embarrassment, insults, and disgrace in front of his wives, his children, and his cousins, Laban's children!

Though he was treated very badly, Jacob couldn't do anything. He just couldn't pack up and leave because of his circumstance; he needed to take care of his family. Laban was fully aware of this and took full advantage of Jacob for his own benefit. Can you imagine what Jacob felt? But the God of justice saw how Laban treated Jacob, and once and for all, God decided to bring justice to Jacob!

God Revealed a Divine Vision to Jacob

> One time during the mating season, I had a dream and saw that the male goats mating with the females were streaked, speckled, and spotted. Then in my dream, the angel of God said to me, "Jacob!" And I replied, "Yes, here I am." The angel said, "Look up, and you will see that only the streaked, speckled, and spotted males are mating with the females of your flock. For I have seen how Laban has treated you."
> (Genesis 31:10–12, NLT)

After divine vision, Jacob renegotiated his wages with Laban.

> Let me go through all your flocks today and remove from them every speckled or spotted sheep, every dark-colored lamb and every spotted or speckled goat... They will be my wages. "Agreed," said Laban. "Let it be as you have said."
> (Genesis 30:32, 34; NIV)

Laban gladly agreed to these terms because he knew animals produced after its own kind. White sheep produces white sheep or black produces black. He knew a sheep of mixed color could only be produced if the sheep is mixed. This was the reason why Laban gladly agreed on these terms.

Then he gathered all the male and female goats that were speckled, spotted, and had some white on it, and all the brown lambs away from Jacob. He put all these animals in the hands of his son's care and sent them off apart from Jacob as far as possible to prevent any of mixed color animals to mate with pure ones.

> So he removed that day the male goats that were speckled and spotted, all the female goats that were speckled and spotted, every one that had some white in it, and all the brown ones among the lambs, and gave them into the hand of his sons. Then he put three days' journey between himself and Jacob, and Jacob fed the rest of Laban's flocks.
>
> (Genesis 30:35–36, NKJV)

Perhaps, Laban thought that Jacob had to be stupid to agree on this term. He may have though he would have more of Jacob's service for nothing and more opportunity to take advantage of Jacob, but what Laban didn't know was that God was involved in this situation.

Jacob continually tended Laban's animals. In Jacob's care, there were no streaked, spotted, white, or dark-colored animals, all pure, but when animals were breeding,

Jacob Acted on Divine Vision

> Now Jacob took for himself rods of green poplar and of the almond and chestnut trees, peeled white strips in them, and exposed the white which was in the rods. And the rods which he had peeled, he set before the flocks in the gutters, in the watering troughs where the flocks came to drink, so that they should conceive when they came to drink. So the flocks conceived before the rods, and the flocks brought forth streaked, speckled, and spotted.
>
> (Genesis 30:37–39, NKJV)

It's very rare that a pure animal would produce a mixed color animal. Jacob knew that peeling bark branches didn't have any power to produce streaked, spotted, and speckled animals. He knew this very well. He was a professional in this area. He was an expert shepherd, but Jacob didn't lean on his experiences, knowledge, or understanding! Instead, he fully trusted God.

He did not consider a divine vision as nonsenses, impossible, or insignificant. By faith! Jacob acted on a divine vision. As Jacob acted on the vision, God caused pure animals to produce mixed animals! Hallelujah! If God leads you to do something, don't depend on your experience, knowledge, or understanding. Trust His lead and follow it. Then you'll see His miracles.

> "Trust in the Lord with all your heart and lean not on your own understanding; In all your ways acknowledge Him, And He shall direct your paths."
> (Proverbs 3:5–6, NKJV)

Jacob increased exceedingly and grew very rich in a short time. Jacob, who had been robbed for twenty years, all of a sudden became extraordinarily rich. God rewarded Jacob for his righteousness and repaid him for the cleanliness of his hands. He arrived at Laban's house with empty hands but became a very rich person. Jacob went through the unfairness of life, but God paid him what was due to him. God is the God of love, but God is also God of justice!

> "Thus the man became exceedingly prosperous, and had large flocks, female and male servants, and camels and donkeys."
> (Genesis 30:43, NKJV)

Addition to Jacob acting on God's unbelievable vision, Jacob never repaid Laban's evil for evil. He could have been vindictive and revengeful, but he didn't. Instead, He remained faithful to God and took care of Laban's flocks as his own.

> These twenty years I have been with you; your ewes and your female goats have not miscarried their young, and I have not eaten the rams of your flock. That which was torn by beasts I did not bring to you; I bore the loss of it. You required it from my hand, whether stolen by day or stolen by night. *There I was! In the day the drought consumed me, and the frost by night, and my sleep departed from my eyes.*
>
> (Genesis 31:38–40, NKJV)

Jacob also could have seriously complained against God. Jacob could have said, "Didn't you promise, you would watch over me? Is this how you watch over me, causing Laban to take advantage over me? You said you will not leave me until you've done what you promised, but where are you? If you are with me, then why am I going through all these unfair situations? I thought you're all powerful? How come you didn't prevent Laban from taking advantage of me?" He could have said all these things, but Jacob remained faithful. He didn't allow any temptations to complained or repay evil for evil.

> "I am with you and will watch over you wherever you go, and I will bring you back to this land. I will not leave you until I have done what I have promised you."
>
> (Genesis 28:15, NIV)

If Jacob took matters into his own hands to pay evil for evil, he would have limited God's powers and justice. But the full power of God manifested to justify Jacob because he didn't take matters into his own hands. He trusted God and obeyed God's way to receive God justice.

Through God's justices, God erased all of Jacob's disgrace and shame. God did not forget about Jacob's good works and love shown for God's name. God saw Jacob's faithfulness, and integrity. His action professed he believed God, and God rewarded Jacob for his righteousness and cleanliness of his hands.

> The Lord rewarded me according to my righteousness; According to the cleanness of my hands He has recompensed me. For I have kept the ways of the Lord And have not wickedly departed from my God. For all His judgments were before me, And I did not put away His statutes from me. I was also blameless before Him, And I kept myself from my iniquity. Therefore the Lord has recompensed me according to my righteousness, According to the cleanness of my hands in His sight.
> (Psalm 18:20–24, NKJV)

Keep your hands clean! God will reward you. Remain faithful to God, not just one day, one week, but be faithful to Him every day. Temptations and challenges will come through anger, bitterness, resentments. Temptation will cause you want to be vengeful.

Your faithfulness will be challenged, tested, and it will be tempted, but don't take matters into your hands. Don't repay them with anger, gossip, backbiting, spitefulness, lying, cheating, stealing, etc. I was tempted by all these negative emotions, but I took it to God.

Don't repay evil for evil. If you repay them with evil for evil, God can't compensate you. God can't bring justice to you because you already receive your own rewards by your evil actions. You made your own reward.

Don't think like a child, don't reason like a child, and don't make a decision like a child. You know what God says about this, do what is right in His sight. He knows what you're going through or went through. He knows you've been taken advantages of by others. God sees everything, notices everything, and hears everything. Your righteousness and faithfulness will be noticed by God.

> He who planted the ear, shall He not hear? He who formed the eye, shall He not see?
> (Psalm 94:9, NKJV)

> And whoever gives one of these little ones only a cup of cold water in the name of a disciple, assuredly, I say to you, he shall by no means lose his reward.
> (Matthew 10:42, NKJV)

God know everything. He even notices a simple cup of water given. How much more will God notice the greater trials you went through or are going through. He knows everything. God will reward and pay you for your righteousness. Keep your hands clean and talk to God honestly, like I did.

Do not hide your true emotions. You shouldn't think, you are not a good Christian because you have hurt feelings. If someone takes advantage of you, feeling hurt is very natural. Don't hide it, oppress it, or try to tolerate it. While carrying all kind of negative emotions, talk to God very honestly about all the hurt emotions, like I did.

You may worry, you might be viewed as a small person or not as a grown Christian to talk to God about it. You see, it is not about you being a small person or a baby Christian. It is all about being truthful to God. God knows it anyway. He knows all of your true feelings. Trust God and let God know your true feelings.

And whatever way He shows you, do it His way. If you endure because you are doing it His way, God will give you your harvest. He will bring your justice in good measure. Take it to God, and not place it in your hands. Be faithful and do what is right before God. For God is the God of love, but God is also the God of justice.

> God is not unjust; he will not forget your work and the love you have shown him as you have helped his people and continue to help them.
> (Hebrews 6:10, NIV)

A bruised reed he will not break, and a smoldering wick he will not snuff out. In faithfulness he will bring forth justice.

(Isaiah 42:3, NIV)

And the heavens proclaim his righteousness, for he is a God of justice.

(Psalm 50:6, NIV)

In His time, His will bring justice for you.

"For the time has come for me to avenge my people, to ransom them from their oppressors."

(Isaiah 63:4, NLT)

As God is alive, His word is alive. And His "Word" will prove to you, He is alive.

23

"Who am I?"
Jehovah Jira

This was the time I was in the ministry as a volunteer pastor. I volunteered with my husband in ministry for a close to two and half years. We led the Asian/American ministry at our local church. We met every Sunday at 5:00 p.m. for about six months, but then our meeting got changed to meet once a month.

We gathered once a month after our main service to eat and fellowship. I was not able to preach nor freely share what God had revealed to me. I got tired of this kind of ministry and lost interest because there was no fulfillment in what God had revealed to me.

I began to pray to God. I asked God to open a new ministry for me. I prayed, "Father, I wish I no longer had to do this type of ministry. I don't think this is not important, but this kind of ministry can be done by anyone. It can be done by whoever has the desire to do this. Father, I want you do open a new ministry for me, but I do not have any means to pay for the rent nor have any members to start a new church."

I let God know what was in my heart and my needs. I further prayed, "Father, next year, April will be three full years that I have volunteered, whether you open up a new ministry for me or not, I will do it until April of next year, but I do not wish to continue after April."

I prayed for a few months for a new ministry, but I didn't know how to start a new church. However, I knew what I needed for a new church. I needed to have money to pay for the rent and buy the things for the new church, like chairs, tables, TV screens for music, and lyrics, and a sound system.

I also knew I needed some members to start a new church. We knew many people from the church that we volunteered at, but as far as we were concerned, they were not our flock. They are the flock that belong to the church we were attending.

I also knew, if I had any bad intentions to start a new church, God would not bless me nor open a new ministry for me. So, I asked God for help in these areas.

As I was a volunteer pastor, same time, I taught the word of God to a sister who lived very close to my house, Lee. (Please read I do not want to teach her anymore). One day, Lee visited me and told me one of her friends was in difficult situation. Lee said whenever she prayed for her friend, God would show her my face. She believed that God wanted me to pray for her friend. I asked, "Does she attend church?"

Lee replied, "Yes, she does."

I asked, "Why can't she ask her pastor to pray for her?"

"He did pray for her," Lee stated, "but somehow, whenever I pray for my friend, God keeps showing me your face. I believe God wants you to pray for my friend."

"Okay if that is the case, I'll go and pray for her."

God Orchestrated

During my first visited to Lee's friend, I went by myself because Lee couldn't go, I'm referring to Lee's friend JJ. JJ owned a small commercial building. Seven units in total. Five units were about nine hundred square feet and two of them were a little bigger. JJ had lots of financial problems. Somehow, she couldn't rent out her units long term to pay her mortgage to the bank.

Tenants did move in, but they all moved out within a few months because they couldn't make any profit in their business. At that time, she only had one space that was rented out, but six other units had been empty for a long time. I prayed and gave her a word of encouragement and left after our first meeting.

About a week later, I received a call from Lee. She asked me to go with her one more time to pray for her friend JJ. Lee told me, JJ told her that she had a very comfortable sleep for a week after I prayed for her. So, JJ made special request to Lee to invite me to pray for her again.

We went and got into one of the business units. We sang a few of hymnal songs and prayed. When we finished praying, JJ asked me, "Why don't you move in here and start a church?"

I asked, "What you are saying?"

She said, "Well, you should move in and start a church. One of the units was going to be rented by a church twice, but something always went wrong. They loved it, but somehow they couldn't rent it out."

Lee and I looked at each other and I said, "Where is it?"

"Right next to this space."

"Okay, let's go and look at it." When we walked into that unit, I had goose bumps all over my body. I just knew that was the place for me to start a new church. So, I asked JJ to do one thing for me. "Sister, would you pray to God for me? Would you pray to God and ask what you can do to help me?" She said she would, then Lee and I left that place.

First Manifestation of an Answer

After that meeting, I changed my prayers. I asked God, if this was the place He wanted me to start a church, then He should reveal His will to JJ. I asked God to touch her heart because I can't afford to pay any rent. About a week later, God strongly urged me to call JJ.

I obeyed and called to see how she was doing. She answered, and we exchanged small talk. Then all of sudden, she said, "Pastor, can you come down here and start a church?"

I told her, "I can't because I can't pay the rent"

Then she said, "Don't you worry about it, just move in and start a church!"

I thought, *What? Okay?* Then I said, "What do you mean?"

She said it again, "Just move in and start a church."

Then I said, "Why don't we meet somewhere to talk about it?"

We met an hour later at Panera Bread restaurant. She said there would not be any contract for me to sign. She just wanted me to move in and start a new church.

She explained her reasons. "It has been unoccupied for long time, and I couldn't make money out of it anyway. For some reason, I can't rent it out. Whether I let you use it or not, it remains an empty space." she said. "At least, if I let you use it for God, perhaps God might bless me through you. For the payment, I want you to pray for me and for my business. That will be the payment."

I realized God started to work on my request. God knew I couldn't make a payment for the rent. She offered me a place to start a church that was rent free. I told her, "Okay, I accept your offer, but I will promise you this. I will pray for you and your business. Additionally, whatever amount of offering God brings into the church, I will pay you according to what we receive. I will pay you whatever amount God speak to my heart." We agreed.

I Was Tempted to Do It My Way

After that meeting, things started moving faster than I expected. I got the place for the church, but I had nothing! No chairs, no sound system, no tables, no pulpit, and not a single member. I had lots of thoughts. I didn't know what I needed to do from that point. Again, I prayed to God. I was still volunteering at the local church we attended, and I was tempted to share this with a few members that we knew from the Asian/American ministry I lead.

I, especially, wanted to share this with one man who was very faithful to the Asian/American Ministry. His name is Mike. Every Sunday when I saw him, I wanted to share with him what God was doing for the new church. God knew, I wanted to share with him for two main reasons. One, I wanted him to join the new church as a starting member, and two, I wanted him to help financially for the church's needs.

So, every Sunday when I saw him, I said, "Hey, Mike, I want to share something with you." Then I heard a warning voice from within my heart. God didn't want me to share. So, I told him, "I will share with you next week." Then following Sunday when I saw him, I tried to share again, but again God stopped me from sharing. So, I had to tell him, "I will share with you next week," but that next week never came.

Although I was tempted to share in order to ask for help financially, I couldn't because God didn't want me to ask anyone for anything. I didn't understand it, but I obeyed God. I just trusted God and prayed. God wanted me to believe He would provide all the new church's needs, but I was wondering how God would accomplish all of this? How?

God's Encouragement

One day, while I was driving to the new church, I found myself having many questions, "Okay, I have a space for the church, but what about everything else? I only had four walls, a ceiling, and the floor. How am I going to provide everything else that's needed?" I was in deep thoughts.

When I almost arrived to the new church, all of a sudden, I heard, "Who am I?" When I heard this, it caught my attention. "Huh?" Then again, "Who am I?" I knew then it was the voice of God. I quickly had many thoughts. "You are my Lord? You are my Father? My savior? My shelter? You are my everything? What are you saying, Father?" I didn't quite understand why He asked, "Who am I?", because He could be all those things that I mentioned above.

Then all of a sudden, I heard, "Am I not Jehovah Jira?"

"???, Oh my god! Yes, you are! You are JEHOVAH JIRA!" How good our Father is! I had a sudden feeling of relief and the joy of the Lord quickly rose within me. I forgot! He is Jehovah Jira! I parked the car, went into the empty church, and began to dance around and sing, "Yes, Lord…yes, Lord, you are Jehovah Jira. Yes, Lord…yes, Lord, you are Jehovah Jira."

From that moment on, I was set free from all those thoughts of how and what was needed for the new church. All the burdens of the unknown had been lifted from me. Right at that moment, I just knew God would provide. I didn't know how God would provide but I knew He would provide. He would do what He says he would do because He is Jehovah Jira!

"Jehovah Jira." Well, I am not going to assume that you know the meaning. In the book of Genesis 21: 4, Abraham was a hundred years old when he received his son Isaac from God. Then in chapter 22, God tested Abraham and asked that he sacrifice his son Isaac as a burnt offering.

I am pretty sure this was not easy for Abraham at all, but Abraham still decided to obey God. Abraham took his son Isaac to region Moriah. He bound Isaac and laid him on the altar on the top of a pile of wood to slay him, but God stopped Abraham from slaying Isaac. Then God asked Abraham to look up to see a ram caught by its horns in a thicket to sacrifice to God instead of Isaac. And there Abraham called this place Genesis 22:14 "Jehovah Jira" meaning, "The Lord Will Provide".

Beginning of the Manifestation of "Jehovah Jira"

After I had finally talked with JJ, a couple weeks later, I met Lee and few other ladies for a Bible study I held weekly. After the Bible study, God urged me to asked Lee for money for the church's needs. As a matter of fact, God told me I should receive $600 from her. I felt so uncomfortable of this because I never ask anyone for money.

She left to do whatever she needed to do, but God continually urged me to ask her. I knew I needed to do it. So, I called her, but she didn't answer. I didn't leave a message. Then a few hours later, she called back and wanted to stop by my house to discuss something.

I was so excited because what God asked me to do all day, I was not able to do, but her coming to my house provided me the opportunity to do it.

She came to my house and we had small talk, and I finally asked her what God told me to ask her. "You know, sister, this is very hard for me to say, but God told me this morning, I should ask you for something."

She asked, "What is it?"

I told her what God had told me to ask. Then she looked up at the ceiling and said, "Lord, I don't have the money."

With that comment, I said, "I understand but God told me to ask you." Then suddenly, she started to laugh. Then she said, "Hold on, hold on for moment, hahaha." With a laugh, she said, "Do you know? When I said to God, I don't have the money, do you know what He said to me? He said, 'No, you do have the money. You have it in your purse.'"

She said, "Oh, sister! I forget. I forget, I do have the money!"

Her story was that she used to own a small convenience store; therefore, she never worked for anyone to receive "a paycheck". At that time, she sold her business and was working for someone else. After starting this job, she made a promise to God that she would give her entire first paycheck to God as a "first fruit" offering.

When she received her first paycheck, she went to her church to give it to God, but for some reason, she didn't want to give it to her church. Since then, she carried it around in her purse for nearly two months. Then she forgot she had that money in her purse, but God reminded her she did have money in her purse.

"Well, I didn't understand why I hesitated to give this first fruit to my church, but now I know. God had a special purpose for this money. Here, sister, I have $400." She handed me the envelope with money inside, and we prayed and thanked God for that offering.

I asked her to hold the money until we go shopping for the church's needs, but something was not quite settled with me because God told me I would receive $600 from her, not $400. I wanted to tell her this, but I didn't because I had some concern that she might change her mind about the $400.

She went to her home, and I was still wondering about the extra $200. "Did I hear God correctly? I know for sure God did say I would receive $600 from her?" But I moved on to prepare dinner. Suddenly, the phone started ringing, and I answered. It was Lee! Without saying a word, she said, "Hey, does the church need a coffee pot?"

"Coffee pot? Yea? We kind of need it during the wintertime, but currently, we really don't need a coffee pot, but why are you asking?"

"Well, after I came home, I called my sister in Korea. I shared what the Lord is doing for your new church. My sister told me she would donate $200 to buy a coffee pot for the church."

Wow, just as God had spoken, $600 from her! Much later, when her sister visited United States, I asked her what caused her to donate $200 for the coffee pot. Coffee pots don't cost $200. A good one may only cost about $30 to $50 dollars. She said that was what she felt to donate to God.

Wow! How amazing God is. It did happen as He told me. Well, from that point on, God brought everything that was needed for the new church. We started with twenty chairs, three tables, a refrigerator, coffee pot, podium, cross, projector, keyboard, sound system, sofa, and many other things we needed. How awesome! He is "Jehovah Jira!"

Four Members

Close to seven weeks had passed and nearly everything was ready for the new worship place. But I still didn't have any church members. One Sunday, when I saw Mike, I wanted to share, not for the money, but for him to join our new church as a member, but once again, God stopped me. So, I told Mike I would share it with him at his house.

He held a monthly home group meeting at his house. The people who attended his meeting were people whom my husband and I knew. I thought, *Perhaps, this might be a better opportunity for me to share. I can share to more people to join with us in our new church. Maybe, this might be the way God want me to share. This may be the reason why God prevent me to share to Mike for this long.*

It was Friday evening. My husband and I went to Mike's house to attend his home group meeting. Before Mike started the meeting, he wanted me to share as I told him I would. Then I heard a warning voice from the inside my heart. I told Mike I would do it after the meeting. After the meeting, once again, I couldn't do it because God didn't want me to do it. I told Mike that I couldn't do. He had a very perplexed look on his face, but I had to hold my tongue.

Then I told God from my heart, "Lord, Mike is going to find out tomorrow. He's supposed to deliver the couch set to the new church tomorrow. He will find it out anyway. Why couldn't I share right now?" But God still didn't want me to share anything to anyone. So, my husband and I left Mike's house without accomplishing what I wanted to accomplish.

The next morning, we met Mike at a lady's place to pick up the couch set for our new church. Mike asked where we were going. I told him just follow us and he would find out shortly. We arrived at the new church and I opened the door. When we brought the couch inside the church, Mike asked, "What is this place?"

I said, "Mike, this is what I've been trying to tell you about for weeks. Every time I tried to tell you, the Lord prevented me."

"I believe, God wanted to show you rather than hearing it from me." I explained to Mike what God was doing for the new church and how God provided all the church's needs.

Then I said, "I have been asking God for some new members to start a church. We really want you to join us as a new member, but we wanted you to hear it from God." I asked Mike to pray to God to hear what God has to say about it. Mike prayed couple of weeks and heard God for himself to join our church as our first member. I'll tell you. God is, "Jehovah Jira!"

Close to our first church meeting, I needed someone to do the final decoration and preparation of the sanctuary. As I was praying for this need, God showed me the face of someone I knew. Her name is Margaret. She is a very faithful woman of God. God gave me a revelation that I could ask her for the decoration.

While God was revealing this to me, He also was placing this desire in Margaret's heart. Prior to me asking her to help with the decorations, Margaret had asked me if she could decorate the multipurpose room we were using at our local church for our monthly Asian/American fellowship.

While this was good idea, I reminded Margaret that since this was a shared space, whatever decorations we set up would need to be taken down at the end of our service. Margaret stated she was perplexed as the room God had shown her was to be decorated long term.

Time had passed by and we had not spoken of this until God has revealed her face to me. So, the following Sunday, I mentioned to her that I needed some help from her, and what day would she be available to help me. She said, "Tomorrow." She asked, "What is it all about anyway?" I told her she would find out if she comes with me.

The next day, which was Monday, we met and drove to the new worship place. When we walked in, she asked, "What is this place?"

I explained to her the entire story and asked, "Can you help me decorate this place? When I prayed, God directed me to ask you to take care of the final decoration."

Then she said, "Oh my god! Do you know what? It has been over a month God showed me an empty room that I needed to decorate. Every time, when I prayed to God, He showed me an empty room that I needed to decorate. I was wondering and tried to figure it out which room He wants me to decorate. Now, I know why God showed me an empty room to decorate!" Without any hesitation, she said, "I will decorate this place as I know this is the will of Father."

That's how she joined us as our second member. God gave us four adults and one child to start the new church. She decorated the church beautifully.

The Lord provided for all our needs, and we launched the new church. God prepared and provided everything for our church. A place for the new worship service, first members, and all the things that the church needed to be established.

How wonderful God is! He is an awesome God! He is "Jehovah Jira!" I didn't persuade anyone to join us nor coax or convincing anyone for one single dollar to start our new church. I didn't do anything considered dishonest, but prayed, listened, and did what God asked me to do and He prove to me that He is "Jehovah Jira!"

He Is Also Your "Jehovah Jira" Too!

I don't know what you've been praying for or waiting on. Don't get discouraged. God is your provider too. He is your "Jehovah Jira!" too. God knows all your needs, just as He knew all of my needs. He will provide everything you need, just believe and trust Him. He already has all the provisions for you even before you make any petition of Him.

> Look at the birds of the air, for they neither sow nor reap nor gather into barns; yet your heavenly Father feeds them. Are you not of more value than they?
> (Matthew 6:26, NKJV)

> For your heavenly Father knows that you need all these things.
> (Matthew 6:32, NASB)

How true this statement is? Birds don't sow nor reap nor gather into barns, but God takes care of them. How much more God cares for you? He will not and does not abandon His children.

He knows all your needs. Just let God know. He knows it before you ask. He just wants you to come and ask Him so that you know it came from Him and not from others. He wants you to know for sure it didn't come from any other source but from God himself. That's the reason why God wants you to ask Him even though He knows what you need. How comforting this word is to us.

> "Ask, and it will be given to you; seek, and you will find; knock, and it will be opened to you"
> (Matthew 7:7, NKJV)

Just ask, God will give to you just as He gave it to me. Once again, He knows all your needs, but He is waiting for you to ask Him. He is your "Jehovah Jira".

As God is alive, His word is alive. And His "Word" will prove to you, He is alive.

About the Author

Pastor Ae Cha Arroyo is the senior pastor of World Harvest Church located in Federal Way, Washington. A native from Inchon South Korea, Ae Cha knew deep in her heart that her life had a divine purpose. God's calling on her life was evident while she was raising her young children in Missouri back in 1991. With the call on her life, she pursued her education first through the University of Maryland, Rhema Bible Training Center and later by graduating from Dominion College in Seattle, Washington. Serving in several ministries at Christian Faith Center in Federal Way, Washington, her desire was to help people from multiple cultures understand that God is real, that He loves them and has a plan for their life. Her passion for the things of God and desire to teach others how to hear and receive from God is evident in her daily walk and teachings. Pastor Ae Cha resides in Auburn, Washington with her husband, Daniel, and their two adult sons, Daniel J. Arroyo and Jeremiah M. Arroyo.

CPSIA information can be obtained
at www.ICGtesting.com
Printed in the USA
FSHW021204091019
62789FS

9 781645 690696